The Intimacy Gram

Distant

DAD → FAMily

Debbie

Familiar

Kathy

KAY

Personal LiSA

DANiel

Mom   DAViD →

MiKE

KAYAKing

←Tony

LeE

DeiAh

Private

GRANDMA
Punky

True Private

KAREN
SheLLy

Miles

2.22/18

LAURiE

KiARA

TRES

Anthony

SheenY

Home

Ken Francis, MS

Ken Francis, MS

ISBN-13: 978-1-9804-5710-7

Names and identifying details have been changed to protect the privacy of individuals.

CONTENTS

Ken Francis, MS

ACKNOWLEDGMENTS

I would like to thank all the interns, colleagues, patients and friends who have inspired me over the last 18 years. You have all helped to shape and expand this concept into what it is today.

The Intimacy Gram

Beginnings

Years back, I led a therapy group for men. This was just a standard, run of the mill support group for guys who needed a forum because they didn't know how to get their needs met. Most had fairly stable lives: work and home. If they had a conflict at work, they might come home and discuss this with the wife or girlfriend. If they had a conflict with the wife or girlfriend, they had nowhere to discuss or process it. Manly men with limited support. Hence, the group.

A totally unrelated women's group transpired next door at the same time every Monday evening. So, every Monday evening, prior to these 2 groups, I would go out to dinner with Karen, leader of the women's group.

Karen's group was somewhat larger than mine. On one such night, while mulling through dinner at the Cypress Cafe, we discussed the difficulty of attracting and maintaining men for a process group. Karen suggested that men aren't as wired for intimacy as women, and thus don't seek out connections with others. I wasn't quite sure I agreed with this. Being a man, I took this personally and felt that she was calling me intimately deficit. I knew I had a capacity for intimacy, challenged as I may be, and I knew the guys in my group truly struggled with the desire for intimacy, but lacked the tools to attain it.

I challenged Karen to let our clients decide this debate. On this night, we asked the members of our group to make a list of the factors of intimacy. We compared lists later that evening.

The answers we saw surprised us. This certainly wasn't a valid clinical study. We didn't have a control group, and the sample numbers were small. A year later with different group members, the outcome might have been different. The important thing I learned that night came out of the richness of the combined lists. My clients had introduced me to a concept that challenged my misunderstanding of what I thought defined intimacy.

The seeds for the Intimacy Gram were planted that night. As my clients continued to struggle with intimacy and balance, this model for diagramming these concepts was created, expanded, and revised.

Over 20 years later, it finally reached print.

The Intimacy Gram

We are the sum of all our relationships and all our experiences. For many of us, our lives are ever-changing. People stream in and out of our lives as we transfer jobs, move on from school, and change our interests and activities. We also let go of one family, start, and embrace another. What we have seen and experienced is who we become. Sometimes our paths lead to joy and serenity, and other times our paths may lead to frustration, anger, and despair.

The quality of our relationships is often a reaction to what we learned early on about interacting with others. As children, we operate as little video recorders: absorbing what we see, hear, and interpret around us. We record our perceptions of our surrounding relationships. We internalize this, and then we play this out in our lives later on. Sometimes, just one incident of trauma can redirect the way we associate with others, change our trust, and completely shape a different path for us. This too can be said for one incident of kindness. At what point do we choose the direction over our own path, making our own choices and empowering ourselves to be who we want to become?

Visual learners conceptualize by seeing material presented before them. This may include pictures, charts, and diagrams. I am a visual person. In this age of global positioning and electronic atlases, I still prefer to use paper road maps. I need to see the "big picture". So, when I wanted my clients in psychotherapy to see the big picture, I put together different models of diagramming communication and socialization. Out of that grew the Intimacy Gram: a way to diagram intimacy and balance. The Intimacy Gram is a *visual* tool to help you see where you are presently on your journey, how the past has affected the course of your path, and what may need to be done to achieve balance in daily living.

Some people like to-do lists. It gives them a visual example of what needs to be done. It also gives a feeling of satisfaction and productivity when crossing off items on the list. The list is most gratifying when everything is displayed as being checked off. *Completion.*

The Intimacy Gram is basically 2 lists. These lists are combined in a single diagram. Items are not "checked off" but may have arrows to show goals of future change.

This book is not so much a "how to change your life book", but it is rather an instruction manual on how to assemble a tool and, later, how to use this tool. This tool helps you to assess the quality of intimacy and balance in your present life. It does not instruct you how to change but will give you a sense of direction based on your assessment. Assembling an Intimacy Gram and combining the two lists is like folding an origami figure. You can use it as a centerpiece, hang it in a window, or toss it in a fire. After seeing the information presented in your completed Intimacy Gram, the *choice and direction* you wish to take is all your own.

The more unbalanced your life is, and the more intimacy you lack, the more useful this tool will be. A completed Intimacy Gram will help you address your spectrum of need.

Map My Life

Thanks goodness for GPS! A smart phone screenshot of a map practically saved my life. I recently drove to Tijuana, Mexico. This was my first time driving myself across the Mexican border. I was alone, and it was 11pm on Cinco de Mayo. I had "map-quested" my destination but was afraid I would lose the signal and the coordinates as soon as I crossed the international border.

Sure enough, my directions disappeared once I lost my U.S. cell phone coverage. I did not lose my satellite signal, so my map continued to work. I knew where I was supposed to go. I just did not know *how* to get there.

Luckily, I had the screenshot of the map with the pinned destination, and I could use that as a reference. I compared the two every few minutes and made my way towards my desired destination. Unfortunately, this was just a reference and not an actual direction, so along the way I accidentally turned down a couple dark, one-way streets, driving against the traffic. This nerve-wracking journey was a learning experience. In the end, I safely made it to my destination.

A completed Intimacy Gram is like the screenshot of my Tijuana road map. Just as a map with a GPS dot shows you where you are in relation to near or distant towns, this diagram displays how distant or intimate you are to your relationships.

A map can be a reference to guide you to where you want to go. An Intimacy Gram gives you the same valuable information to set you on a course of action and change. Even if you are uncertain of what direction you wish to go in life, the Intimacy Gram will show you your options. It does not necessarily reveal the route to take you there. This is open to your own interpretation, and you might learn as I did that there are sometimes one-way streets along the way that you will want to avoid.

The Intimacy Gram is a *therapeutic visual tool*. An initial diagram will show you how connected you are to the relationships around you. It will also show you which areas of your life are in balance, and which are imbalanced. The rich information presented gives awareness. This awareness can be put into action for positive growth and direction.

On a journey, we might open a map to see how far we have come, how far we have left to travel, or to see our route options. Obstacles blocking our way may also cause us to reassess and reroute. We might even wake up to realize someone else has the steering wheel and we are not traveling on our journey of choice.

We travel through life and we change. Our circumstances change. Redoing an Intimacy Gram every few months helps us stay focused and moving in the right direction.

The Intimacy Gram in Real Life

Rob was an intern therapist working with children and families. He was completing the process of necessary tasks for his state counseling license. Unfortunately, he was experiencing burn out before his career officially began.

Rob had some college friendships but felt most of his friendships had grown stale. He complained to his co-workers about his hopelessness in working with his patients. "They are depressed families and have no hope. I have lost my hope in any change for them". He left work drained and in his own despair. Each day felt like stepping onto a hamster wheel, and he could not see a way off.

I worked with Rob and explained to him the various factors of intimacy, life realms, and how to draft an Intimacy Gram.

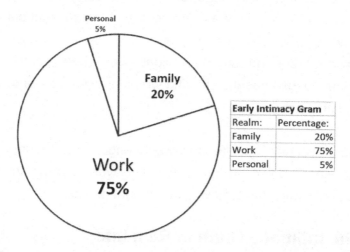

Early Intimacy Gram	
Realm:	Percentage:
Family	20%
Work	75%
Personal	5%

The first thing that stood out for Rob was the imbalance in realms, the social areas in his life. Time not spent at work was spent with his mother and three younger sisters. He realized that he wasn't spending as much time with friends as he thought. As the oldest in his family, he struggled to be the successful son who his parents wanted him to be. But the cost of vocational success included a deficit of self-care and lack of a healthy nurturing support system outside of his family.

Another missing piece in his imbalanced life was the lack of a healthy sense of spirituality. Rob lacked a positive and hopeful connection with the world around him. Relationships lacked the fundamental factors of intimacy. He could only see his glass as half empty and lost sight that at least he had a glass.

Rob realized that his family and clients pulled life force from him. He lacked the balance of people in his life to help lift him up and give him a sense of positive connection. He needed activities and connections with friends to give him a positive sense of "recharging" or invigorating his spirit. Rob targeted this as the first steps in creating balance and intimacy.

Later Balance in Realms	
Realm:	Percentage:
Work	60%
Family/Home	15%
Personal	5%
Outdoors Club	20%

Outdoors Club 20%

Personal 5%

Work 60%

Family/Home 15%

In short, Rob worked on creating new social realms where he could meet positive and potential friends. He joined an outdoors club and challenged himself physically, mentally and socially by taking longer and more strenuous hikes. He began feeling a connection with nature and started to see himself as part of a bigger picture. This gave him a new perspective on his family and career, and more choices in possible directions for personal satisfaction.

What Intimacy is Not: Misconceptions About Intimacy

Most people have a preconceived notion of what intimacy is, and a very limited view. They are not aware of the spectrum and nuances involved in an intimate relationship. Many who operate under this limited view may have somewhat unfulfilling relationships and do not understand why. Four common preconceived ideas about intimacy are: intimacy is all-or-nothing closeness, intimacy is sex, intimacy is based on loyalty, and love alone determines intimacy.

These beliefs about intimacy are learned. They come from parents or authority figures when we are young. The messages may be implied or taught directly. We absorb these messages as truth and then operate accordingly.

Intimacy is All-or-Nothing: Are you in, or are you out? Are you searching for your soulmate, like what comes out of a Hollywood happy ending? Intimacy is a broad spectrum made up of several components. We grow up with fairy tales and movies, and strive for that "perfect" relationship. When we don't get the "happily ever after", we settle or abandon. We do this because we don't analyze the nuances in the relationship and try to support what is working, nor do we try to improve areas of intimacy where are lacking.

If we come from a family whose ties are based on criticism and conditional love, it is easy to see people as either good or bad. We adopt and internalize early messages from a dysfunctional family of origin. In essence, we adopt the critical voice we once despised, and we judge others conditionally. When others do not meet up to our standards or "conditions", we focus on the negative. We either suffer in a relationship we see as all bad or move on without viewing the relationship for the strengths or positives it may possess. It is easy for some to base their relationships on ideals, and as soon as ideals are lacking, move on from the relationship without the patience to do work on acceptance and communication.

Intimacy is Sex: The first person most people think of when asked who they are intimate with is their sexual partner. On the broader scale, most will think of the significant sexual partners that they have had in their life. This discredits all the intimate relationships had with other significant people throughout life, such as the non-sexual intimacy shared with parents, children, best friends, and so forth.

Intimacy is NOT sex. Sex is just *one* factor among many others that may help contribute to a deeper level of connection within a relationship. "20 minutes does not make a relationship" after all.

Sex by and of itself does not necessarily contribute to intimacy. Relationships that are based on sex may hold a lot of fun and passion. This fun and passion may also fill a purpose or a need. Riding a roller coaster or parachuting out of an airplane may fill a passion or a need too, but these are *activities* and not necessarily interactions with others that ever transcend to a deeper level. Relationships based on sex may grow into a deeper level of intimacy if other factors are explored and nurtured.

Intimacy is based on Loyalty: This refers to the statement, "blood is thicker than water." In some cultures, the rule is "Family First." There is an unwritten code of loyalty within the family. Right or wrong, you stand with your family. With this belief, loyalty comes first and foremost. It may be a code for operating within the family, but it is not necessarily a foundation for intimacy. It might also undermine intimacy in other areas of your life.

Familial loyalty may actually contribute to exclusivity within a family; not allowing others to join and be intimate. Marrying into a family with tight, loyal bonds may require relinquishing ties with one's family of origin. The loyalty of one's family is placed above and beyond all others, not allowing for compromise or the melding of families.

Love Alone Determines Intimacy:

Love is but one of many factors in the intimacy spectrum. Love is attachment and desire. This is tricky as we can be attached to people we may love but do not like, and we can desire people we are not in love with. *Love, by and of itself, does not determine intimacy.* It determines love. Love is blind. It often gives us an illusion of intimacy by minimizing or ignoring the other factors of intimacy. We may fail to see past missing factors of intimacy. We may also exaggerate other factors in the hope that they might be so.

Love drives us. It can be a sense of belonging, and we can also make our love our identity. This driving factor can reach addiction proportion when given the power to be our sole driving factor.

Attachment is a strong internal mechanism. We are programmed for attachment at birth. This is how we survive. This mechanism can be damaged in early formative years, allowing people to be easily and constantly in a state of attachment, or diminishing the ability for attachment with another.

Love with the absence of other factors of intimacy can be a

recipe for a disaster. In some relationships, love may keep us in denial as to the true levels of intimacy in the relationship. The desire for attachment, and the need to attach for identity, fuels the denial process. We fail to see the "big picture." We may love someone and yet feel totally empty and unfulfilled. Some remain in relationships like this for several years; others may wake up and sense the disillusionment. Without correcting the overall view of intimacy, this type of attachment based on love will be repeated in the next relationship.

Transient Intimacy

Often times we experience connections that seem instantaneous. People we may have recently met might feel like someone we have known for years. There is a sense of familiarity/comfort and identification, e.g. "You like Chinese food? I like Chinese food, too!" Identification is strong initially, only to be followed by lack of identification and let down. This is a seductive and transient form of intimacy. It is also a trap. Intimacy is not instant identification.

Think of the difference between sitting across from somebody in a large, harshly lit cafeteria, or sitting across a small table from somebody in a dimly lit bistro. On the surface, the candlelight dinner appears much more intimate. The stranger you see occasionally at the cafeteria, might become your friend someday and you may realize that you have several factors in common. The person with you in the bistro might be pleasant company, but the moment is created by the atmosphere and not necessarily the interpersonal chemistry. Intimacy can be enticing and deceptive, and it is ever-changing.

The early stages of most relationships usually begin with connecting on common points. Identification is not intimacy. There is a trap in instant over-identification, especially if this is a person we *wish* to connect with, either through physical or intellectual attraction. Once the initial attraction wears off, so does the comfort and identification, e.g. "I like Chinese food, but NOT EVERY NIGHT!" The relationship flips from working towards commonalities to seeing a more complete picture of the other person, which now includes everything that you do not have in common.

Transient relationships are usually based on some element of passion, and as quickly as they become intense, they eventually lose their meaning. Sometimes despair, rejection, and abandonment follow. People with a long pattern of these relationships also will doubt their own self-worth if they question why they cannot maintain their relationships. In reality, these relationships were destined to fail due to the lack of elements, or factors, of intimacy.

Some relationships are just transient in nature. Actors in community theater go from show to show. Traveling nurses have varied assignments that take them to different cities.

15

Therapists may work with patients intensely, but for a limited time. Players on a bowling league or soccer team may only be together for one season. These all represent relationships that may bring people together for shared celebrations or defeats; intense experiences that are time limited. People often discuss staying in contact afterwards, but follow-through is rare, or dissipates.

Transient relationships are problematic when you cannot accept them for what they are. Feeling a loss after they end is understandable but personalizing the loss and carrying this with you may prevent you from getting close to others in the future.

Non-Reciprocated Relationships

Relationships rarely mirror each other with the same factors of intimacy, meaning that one person's list of factors for another may not look like the other's factors towards that person. In most relationships, one person may be slightly more nurturing than the other, but the other person may balance this out with another factor. This is the part that *chemistry* plays in a relationship. Balance is maintained due to overall reciprocity.

There are a few healthy relationships where intimacy is present, but not reciprocated. These relationships include those with doctors, lawyers, teachers, and therapists. It could also include the relationship with an AA, NA, or ACA sponsor.

In these relationships, intimacy is fairly one-way. This is due to the design of the relationship. The professionals in these relationships need to maintain a level of objectivity. This objectivity is what creates the environment for growth or satisfactory outcomes.

In order for these professional relationships to work, a person needs to develop trust, compassion, and understanding, along with a certain level of vulnerability, and do so without expecting much reciprocity from the professional.

If the relationship with the professional becomes more balanced, than objectivity is threatened. The goals of getting care from the professional is also jeopardized if the focus switched to the professional trying to get their needs met from those they are helping (poor boundaries).

Non-Intimate Relationships

Relationships with objects or rituals are not intimate. This may include a relationship with your car, your garden, your hobby, or your favorite sport. These might be recreational items, but intimacy is about connecting with another being. These things make up realms in your life. These realms are generally populated with other individuals: friends and family who share the common interests. It is the relationship with others *within* the realm that constitutes intimacy.

If a relationship to an object feels intimate, the relationship may be on a spiritual level. This is generally how we connect with a compulsion, obsession, or addiction. We may feel a sense of fulfillment from engaging with the object and its associated rituals. The danger exists when the relationship is consuming, such as the relationship to your phone (texting) while having dinner with friends (avoiding). These relationships usually do not contribute to balance, healthy functioning, or intimacy with others.

Understanding the Intimacy Gram:
10 Components

Drafting an Intimacy Gram consists of understanding and executing the following 10 components:

1. Factors of Intimacy
2. Levels of Intimacy
3. Realms
4. Anchors
5. Initial Charting
6. Assessment
7. Planning/Action
8. Ghost Relationships
9. Hats and Masks
10. Maintenance

1: Factors of Intimacy

The first step in building an Intimacy Gram is defining the concept of intimacy and identifying the various factors involved.

At face value, *intimacy is closeness*. Lack of intimacy, therefore, is a void of personal connection. *But how do we connect?* The "closeness" of intimacy is based on several factors. Being able to identify the ingredients involved in intimate relationships helps build an understanding of the various intimate traits in each of our personal and unique relationships.

The ingredients, or *factors of intimacy*, are like colorful interlocking toy building bricks. If you go to the store to buy a box of building bricks, they are sold in a variety of sets. Some come boxed with hundreds of pieces with a large spectrum of shapes and sizes. Some boxed sets have few pieces, and a very limited amount of variation among the pieces.

Each relationship we have contains different types of factors of intimacy, and varying degrees of the amount of each factor. In essence, each of our relationships is like a box containing different shaped and colored building bricks; some may have lots of variety, and others may have just a few colors or shapes. Some boxes may be close to being empty. Boxes with the most bricks are the most complex, and because of the complexity, no two boxes will have the exact same content.

Unlike the boxed sets you get at the store, you have the ability to sort through your boxes and see what pieces work or don't work. If you take inventory and see that desired pieces are missing, it is possible to work on adding those pieces, those factors of intimacy, to your box/relationship.

With the right building bricks, you can build a project. With the right factors of intimacy, you can build a strong relationship. Understanding these elements is important in analyzing relationships in order to strengthen and improve them.

The following list represents contributions from dozens of Intimacy Gram workshops. These are the most common factors of intimacy brought up by workshop participants. Think of this as an master inventory of the building bricks available for your relationship building needs:

- Acceptance
- Accessibility/Availability/Proximity
- Accountability
- Affection/Touch
- Authenticity
- Balance
- Being in the Moment
- Care and Concern
- Chemistry

- Comfort
- Commitment
- Communication
- Compassion/Kindness
- Compatibility
- Compromise
- Confidence
- Empathy
- Encouragement/Challenge
- Equity
- Forgiveness
- Gratitude/Appreciation
- Healthy Boundaries/Interdependence
- History
- Honesty
- Humility
- Identification
- Interdependence
- Kinship/Compatibility
- Love
- Loyalty
- Mutual Attraction
- Open-mindedness
- Passion
- Patience
- Physical Attraction
- Playfulness
- Recognition

- Reliability
- Respect
- Risk
- Romance
- Security
- Sex
- Shared Background/Experiences/Community
- Shared Beliefs
- Shared Goals
- Shared Humor
- Shared Interests
- Shared Intellectual Level
- Shared Values
- Sincerity
- Stability
- Support
- Surrender
- Sympathy
- Teamwork/Unity
- Tolerance
- Transparency
- Trust
- Understanding
- Value
- Validation
- Vulnerability
- Willingness

If you can understand the factors, or the *pieces*, of intimacy, you can also identify the pieces that may be *missing* in important relationships.

"Damn, this Lego set is missing an important piece!"

Growth may come from adding missing pieces to a relationship or strengthening it by adding more of existing pieces. Not all pieces are necessary in all relationships. Not all relationships share the same depths and intensities.

This list is a comprehensive compilation accrued over many years of seminars. Some of these factors may be similar to other factors, and some are very unique and important. Factors that are similar, or "shades" of a common concept, may be culturally based. This list may also vary from culture to culture based on cultural norms, and acceptance of these norms. There are certainly several core factors involved in *truly intimate* relationships.

Ken Francis, MS

Two of the most important factors to understand are *Communication* and *Trust.*

Communication: The Factor that Holds it all Together

A house is only as strong as its foundation. Walls will lean and crack if the foundation is not strong and stable. The roof will not stay up if the walls are not firm and stable. A relationship is the same way. Communication is the one factor that supports every other factor in building a relationship. This factor is key to any relationship. Other factors, such as respect, affection, support, security, and love, all have a component of communication in them. If you cannot communicate these factors, they cannot exist.

Communication is the process of sending and receiving information. It is also acknowledgment and clarification that this information is sent and received properly. We communicate in several ways. Actions speak louder than words, and an absence of communication can speak volumes.

Verbal communication is but one form in which we exchange information. We may also communicate through behaviors: eye contact, touch/affection, tone, and mannerisms, as well as with an absence of these traits.

Communication is such an important factor in intimacy that if you are not a good communicator you will most likely lack intimate relationships.

Trust: Understanding a Spectrum, and Not an Absolute

A strong sense of trust is not always necessary in a relationship, However, understanding and accepting the existing level of trust is very important. Trust is not an absolute, or *all-or-nothing*. We may trust a babysitter with our children, yet not trust them to work on our car. We might trust our auto mechanic with the car, having comfort in believing the brakes will work and tires will be installed properly, and yet we might not trust this person with our children. It becomes about knowing *when*, *where*, and *how far* to trust.

Some people believe that they simply "can't trust anyone". They see the world as black-and-white, no shades of gray. They define themselves with insecurity, trust no one, and live a "me against the world" set of defenses. These people openly state they have trust issues and defy guidance from bosses, sponsors, or others in authority. They make *not trusting* a part of their identity. These people fail to realize the trust they have on a daily basis, such as trusting that opposing traffic at an intersection will stop while they go through a green light, or trusting that a cashier properly rung them up without checking the receipt. This is not to say that some do not have difficulty with trust and intimate relationships, but rather it is almost impossible to have absolutely no trust whatsoever.

Trust might be specific amongst realms or roles. You can have faith that your best friend will help you move from home to home, but this friend might work in a different profession, and not be someone to confide in regarding professional guidance. You might trust a fellow kayaker to save your life if you tip over, but off the water, this might not be someone you would trust. When we see trust as all-or-nothing, we only set ourselves up for disappointment, feelings of abandonment, and heartache. Accepting the trust that exists in your role with another, or within your shared realm, will help you accurately place your relationship within the proper level of intimacy.

And then there's Love...

Love is a tricky word in the English language as it defines a range of heartfelt feelings: love for your fellow man, love for your neighbor, brotherly/sisterly love, romantic love, parental love, and spiritual love. In English, we throw this into one word. When thinking about *love* as a factor of intimacy, it is good to know which definition you are referring to for each individual relationship.

Love does not magnify the other factors. If anything, it has a tendency to overlook deficits as well as intimacy killing factors. Some people remain in abusive or toxic relationships because love is a primary factor that masks the absence of other factors.

Passion, which is different than love, may appear to *magnify* other factors of intimacy. Passion can be a deceiving factor of intimacy. It can be immediate or demand instant gratification. Love, after a while, may actually give a sense of decrease in passion and other factors as we shift from the immediacy of passion to love.

Not on Common Ground

For many, the concepts of communication, trust, and love can be very confusing, if not *overwhelming*. Other factors from the comprehensive list might be equally as baffling, overwhelming, or feared. It depends on your frame of reference. Some have grown up in households where most, if not all, of the factors of intimacy were not present or modeled. If this was the case, we learned about these concepts by watching those around us. This was how we developed our belief system, values, confidence, and self-esteem.

Most of us have been brought up in a very complicated world

and felt a deficit in some of the listed factors. We have experienced some form of separation, abandonment, rejection, or trauma. This may have come from emotional, physical, or sexual abuse in our family of origin, or something simpler like being bullied on the playground or left behind to repeat a grade while your peers progressed. These experiences shaped us. What we learned, or didn't learn, about factors such as security, patience, respect, value, and compassion might be different than what others have learned. We might also have tried to "fill in the blanks" or over compensate for what we were not taught. Certainly, the experiences and understanding of intimacy vary between us all.

Some of us report no apparent trauma or grief while growing up. Many without any identifiable trauma will still marvel at the vastness of the Factors of Intimacy list, and at closer glance, will spot factors weak or missing from their life.

In working on your Intimacy Gram, you may find confusion or lack of understanding of several of these factors. These "building blocks" may have never been in any of your boxes. Realizing this may lead to further self-exploration and an education in factors never learned.

Affection is a factor that stands out with many who I work with. They acknowledge this was not present in their home or culture while growing up, and they struggle to nurture and connect with their own children.

For some, reading the Factors of Intimacy list is like finding out that there are other letters in the alphabet. Attaining new letters creates the formulation of new words in an expanding vocabulary. Or... It can be like going to the building block store and getting shiny new bricks to create something new.

2: Levels of Intimacy

Categorizing the Strengths of Relationships

For the Intimacy Gram, varied closeness of intimacy is broken down into 5 distinct levels. The levels are True Private, Private, Personal, Familiar, and Distant. These levels of intimacy are categories which help establish a reference point to how close someone is to you. Each level also represents different traits in relationships. The relationship and intimacy we have with someone at one level will be characterized by traits we may not see with someone in a different level.

If you can think of each person in your life as an individual box of building bricks, the five levels of intimacy represent a five-level categorization. Think of 5 levels like a shelving unit with 5 shelves. The boxes containing the fewest building bricks are stored on the very bottom shelf. The bottom shelf is packed full of many casual relationships. Those containing a few more pieces are stored on the shelf above. We naturally have fewer boxes the higher we go.

There is no exact formula for determining how different factors of intimacy, how many factors, and the quality of these factors, add up to each level. This is not scientific or a math equation.

Determining the level where a relationship falls is a personal formula that needs to be balanced and consistent among all relationships. Listing the 5 to 10 closest people to you and ranking them in order, may be a good basis on which to start. This creates a reference point for all other relationships.

For simplistic reasons, the 5 levels of intimacy are broken down into equal parts. Each represents 20% of the entire spectrum. With the spectrum equaling 100%, Distant makes up the bottom 20%, followed by Familiar at 20-40%, Personal at 40-60%, Private at 60-80%, and topping it off, True Private at 80-100%. This range of 0% to 100% includes the absolute absence of intimacy to that which is deep and all-encompassing.

True Private ~ 80-100%:

At the top of the spectrum sits the True Private level of intimacy. This level is characterized by the concepts of *spirituality*. It is a closeness so intensely personal that it signifies relationships in a unique category of intimacy.

Spirituality represents the pinnacle of personal relationships, and the closest connection possible. Spiritual relationships transcend time, space, and the physical world. For this reason, it is unrealistic to place living adults in this level of intimacy (with one possible exception).

Extreme closeness is something most of us desire. Searching for that closeness makes this the area where most people are trying to fit others, only to be left feeling unfulfilled and let down. We are trying to fill a void that cannot be filled by another living person/adult. This is where we seek to place our "soulmates" and achieve our happily-ever-after. If there was such a thing, it would go here. Unfortunately, relationships like this would be beyond perfection. Perfection does not exist in relationships as all relationships have their challenges, struggles, and imperfections. With time and circumstances, even the strongest of relationships need to recalibrate. And "perfection" can become boring with time. *Note: If you have found a perfect soulmate, free of conflict and full of complete intimacy, there is a strong likelihood that you will not be reading this book.*

The following are relationships that may fall under the distinction of being spiritual. These examples are ideals, and might not actually be in your True Private while in early stages of healing or recovery.

- Your Higher Power
- Your infant
- Your pets

- People who have passed
- Your drug of choice (or other compulsion)
- Your identical twin

Your Higher Power - God, Jesus, Buddha, Muhammad, Allah, the sky, the wind and trees; this is your internal connection to the Universe. Some people feel connected to science, or to the love they feel surrounding them. Whatever the connection is, this connection brings with it a sense of *belonging*. It helps us to feel a part of a bigger picture. Intimacy exists when you have a relationship with this belief. For some, this is the ultimate connection. A strong faith in the belief of a Higher Power can offer strength and hope. It can help to balance and manage all other relationships.

Your Higher Power doesn't necessarily go into the True Private level of intimacy automatically. Your relationship with your Higher Power can fall anywhere in the spectrum of closeness. This is certainly a relationship, or a *walk*, that must be worked at. It can be the foundation of your humility.

Infants - The parental bond between a parent and infant is spiritual. The child is a part of the parent, and the parent is an extension of the newborn. This relationship grows less spiritual as the child grows and develops into an individual, requiring more than basic needs and having an expanded personality.

Pets - A close relationship with a pet can be both spiritual and therapeutic. For elderly or single people, the daily relationship with a pet may establish the closest relationship with another living being. Pets may create a symbiotic relationship and a sense of purpose. Dogs pull us outside for walks. Cats want to snuggle. Dogs, cats, and birds require interaction, and may be able to read and respond to our emotions. It is this heightened level of communication and interaction that make these relationships spiritual.

For some, pets are sole companions. Factors of intimacy might be heightened with the absence of few personal connections with other people. This may be the deepest level of companionship in someone's life. It is important to remember that loss of such a companion becomes extremely difficult, if not catastrophic.

People who have passed - We hold onto emotions and memories of loved ones who have passed. The relationship we hold with these people becomes internalized. Spiritual. We hold these people in our hearts for many years. We may talk to these people, and even feel their presence. We keep them with us, close to our heart, and they continue to influence and inspire us. Because of this, the relationship lives on. It is current, on a spiritual level.

Addictions and compulsions - Self-defeating rituals and dependencies can deceptively be your higher power. Food, alcohol, sex, gambling, compulsive shopping, television, and codependency/caretaking of others can be your driving force. This force binds you to the relationship with your "drug" and brings this relationship to a spiritual level.

When an addiction or compulsion fills the spiritual level on an Intimacy Gram, there is little room for true intimacy with others.

Addictive behaviors become sacred rituals. These rituals are priority and become protected at all costs. In 12-Step Recovery, this relationship brings the need of a Higher Power in Step 2 to replace the control of the addiction. 12-step programs intend to implement new, healthy rituals to replace the power and influence of the old ones.

The relationship you may hold with cigarettes may appear simple, but you could organize your daily structure around this relationship. You may even carry your cigarettes with you in a pocket close to your heart. You may strain relationships with those who do not like the smell or who are allergic to the smoke. At a deep level, you protect this addictive relationship rather than tend to the relationships you have with the people around you.

Television can be said to be the "drug with the plug". Some people fall into a vortex and make TV/cable/internet/social media a very important and time-consuming part of their lives. Even with the advent of DVR, people can place sitting in front of their television a priority. It even has the label "binge watching". This can be a real intimacy-killer.

A Relationship with an Identical Twin - Sharing genetics, as well as time in the womb, creates a bond that few understand. The communication between these twins may be inter-psychic, bordering on spiritual.

Identical twins often mirror and complement each other. One twin might make up for strength in an area the other is lacking. Twins may take on their own roles, e.g. where one is more emotional and the other is more cognitive, or thoughtful. This creates a balance between the two that makes them one complete individual.

Problems in balance occur when one twin moves on with their life, and the other is not ready to individuate or let go. The same can be said when an identical twin passes. It is usually impossible to ever gain the same depth and connection that one had with their twin, and this can affect intimacy with all other relations.

Private ~ 60-80%:

This is where you find your most valued and fulfilling intimate relationships. These are the richest relationships and the closest you can be to someone shy of a spiritual existence. Once again, these and other examples represent ideals and may not actually represent the status of current relationships.

Each relationship at this level of intimacy is like a box of building blocks filled with large amounts of several of the factors. Not all the factors might be present, but usually there is a deep history characterized by trust, communication, honesty, respect, and love. Other factors usually exist as well, and with strength. Here you would typically wish to place your spouse, your best friend, and possibly your parents or your children. Twins may share intimacy at this level and may sometimes approach the intimacy found in True Private.

These relationships are generally fostered over a period of time. Initial attractions, likes, and similarities are explored, expanded upon, adapted, and compromised. Private level relationships have been worked on, established, and maintained. Those whom you share this closeness with have usually shared your trials. Heartaches, disagreements, triumphs, and joys line the past with these people. The closeness here is characterized by *strength* and *acceptance*.

Personal ~ 40-60%:

Good friends and *close family relationships* fill this level of intimacy. These are the people who are ingrained in your life. They may be a part of your daily structure or be involved in family rituals and traditions. People with solid, healthy relationships may place siblings and cousins at this level. Some people work in environments where they rely on and trust their coworkers in everyday life. Examples of this would be steelworkers, policemen, firefighters, teachers, and emergency room personnel. The interdependence with these long-time coworkers might create special friendships and alliances. The comfort and security with these relationships would place them at the Personal level.

Few relationships have the richness to progress beyond this level. *Factors of intimacy* at this level are comfortable, and to go beyond would require much transparency, trust, energy, and *desire to do so.*

Familiar ~ 20-40%:

These relationships have enough common factors to make them stronger than acquaintances, yet are still very casual and lack the depth of the levels above it. Names like "fair-weather friends" and "casual relationships" typify relationships at this level. There may be comfort, familiarity, consistency, but no depth in these relationships. Examples may include friends on a bowling league, co-workers who lunch together, people who fellowship over dinner following a 12-Step meeting, or neighbors in a community.

Sometimes close relationships fade. Lives go in different directions, and levels/factors of intimacy change. You might not be as close to a friend as you were in college. Siblings may move across the country and grow apart. Placing someone at this level does not invalidate the past closeness, but rather acknowledges the present closeness and status of the relationship.

Distant ~ 0-20%:

This level is characterized by acquaintances or by severed, neglected, or damaged relationships. This may include co-workers, people at the gym, your postal carrier, AA peers, or classmates at school. This level is the "bottom shelf" where you store your most empty building-brick boxes. This may be a point of entry, or exit, for some.

Relationships have to start somewhere. Strangers get to know each other, begin to identify with each other, and the intimacy process begins. Some of the people around us are so distant that we fail to think about them when listing our associates.

As stated earlier, we grow apart from others at different points in our life. One-time close relationships may become toxic, stressed, or detached from the factors that made them more intimate in the past. As we purposely distance ourselves from others, or naturally drift apart, we decrease the factors of intimacy and end up in the lower level, distant or estranged. Almost gone but not forgotten.

Distant is by far the level where we have most of our relationships. Sometimes we know these people by name, sometimes we don't. We may know their profession, some history, the kind of mood they are generally in, but we don't usually think of these people when they are out of sight.

The box of building blocks here is fairly empty to very empty. Classifying someone as distant doesn't really represent the quality of the individual, but rather the lack of factors of intimacy. People in this area may be available for more of an intimate relationship, but the energy and time placed on the relationship is not present. Or there may be a fear of intimacy keeping the relationship at this level.

We may interact with people in the Distant level daily or we may have infrequent contact with them. Contact, proximity and availability are factors of intimacy that hold little closeness by and of themselves.

People in this level of intimacy may have held a place in a closer level at another time. Our lives change. Things that we value or focus on change. Friendships have their seasons. Think of your close friends from high school, the best man at your wedding, your first love, previous neighbors, and the people with whom you carpooled to work for many years. Lives take different directions. The relationships, although they may have become more detached and distant with time, still exist.

3: Realms

Realms are the primary areas of your present-day life. These are the different "worlds" that you pass through from day to day, week to week, or month to month. Each realm is made up of its own structure. This structure is defined by rituals and routine. The structure in each individual realm gives that realm a specific focus. For most people who work 40 hour a week jobs, work can be the biggest realm in their life. Other realms can include school, church, family, and support groups. Realms can give us a sense of belonging, and usually serve financial, spiritual, recreational, medical, legal, or social needs.

Our realms also represent the different hats we wear in our life, and sometimes the different masks that we use. We pass through different realms as we go about our daily lives, sometimes shifting between them as casually as one might pass from one room to the next. Other times we enter a realm with anxiety, fear, and resistance. Realms might also not always be clearly defined, as the people we populate in each realm might be present in more than one specific realm.

Think of your life as a pie, and the realms in your life represent the different slices. Your slices are most likely not going to be equal in size. Please remember, you have one whole pie, not 2 pies, or half a pie. Your life adds up to one entire pie, so all

Realms: How You Slice

Bowling

Work

Personal

On-line Shopping

Home

School

Friends and Family

Church

Your Pie

your slices must be combined to form this one pie. The pie represents 100% of your time.

Too many slices might represent being over extended or stressed. Too many slices might also mean that each slice is very thin. A multitude of slices could represent that you never have time to fully devote to any single slice. Little time means you are moving onto the next realm as soon as you arrive. It is difficult to feel anchored and connected when your life is spread amongst so many realms. *"Hello, I must be going".* Traveling amongst so many realms could create a lack of time to ever develop and sustain true intimacy with anyone.

What represents having *too many* realms? The absence of time to fully devote exactly what is needed into each of the realms. Also important is the *personal realm* that allows you the time to digest and decompress from all other realms. Too many realms also create a rush from realm to realm, which leads to stress and imbalance. Life becomes about catching up. Unchecked stress leads to unhealthy behaviors and health problems, as well as emotional isolation.

Time spent sleeping is not represented or included in this model. Sleep is an important element of self-care and lack of sleep can certainly make your pie completely out of balance.

People who are extroverts might thrive on having several realms. They feel energized and recharged by always having somewhere to go and something to do. This leads to a strong sense of structure and fulfillment. For extroverts, this is a preferred lifestyle. It might work for them.

Introverts, people who are drained by too much time with others, may need a bigger "personal slice", or time alone, to regroup and recharge.

Wanting to "do it all", beyond reason, leads to being over extended. While some people choose this and have some success at managing, there is a trap and risk of being spread too thin. This is true when realms don't start out this way but become more demanding of time and effort. Due to the lack of time and availability, relationships suffer.

Too few realms can lead to isolation and despair. Realms need to give us a sense of fulfillment. There are some who are happy keeping their life simple, with few realms. They have purpose and are fulfilled. These people usually have their realms filled with a high level of purpose and enriching relationships. Others withdraw into a life of few realms, only to be depressed and dissatisfied.

Living in despair: Some people yearn to have fulfilling realms complete with warm friendships, but they may lack the skills, confidence, and energy/mood to attain this. Fear of intimacy may also keep someone bound to an unfulfilled life. These people are trapped in a pie with very few slices and very few relationships. Depression and low self-esteem can be a non-productive means to an end. Charting a *desired* Intimacy Gram may be a tool to help somebody in this situation gain direction and be able to take baby steps to moving out of isolation.

Purpose of Realms – Simply put, realms give us a sense of purpose and fulfillment and they do this by providing consistency; structure and ritual.

Healthy realms keep our life in balance. They provide coping skills, support, direction, self-care, and equity in complementing of other realms. When our realms are balanced and healthy, we are happy and fulfilled. We are also content in our direction and have satisfaction at the end of the day.

A Wheel in Motion - Some of us are used to tension. We grew out of environments where the norm, or homeostasis, existed at a certain level of stress. Sometimes this stress was chaos, other times it was just a certain level of tension, fear, or uncertainty. If we are accustomed to having our own homeostasis include a bit of stress, this becomes familiar, and our norm. We might recreate this stress in our family, or we might choose demanding professions which also have this familiar level of stress. We may even complain about our stress but keep perpetuating the norm. In this sense, we keep ourselves stuck in the ongoing tension and chaos.

Not everyone is accustomed, or desensitized, to living with tension. Some have already worked at eliminating undue stress and drama from their lives. These people function under a different "normal".

A wheel can still spin even if it is not in perfect round or perfect balance. The question is; *are we destined to remain on a bumpy ride?*

Types of Realms

Realms provide us with the structure and motivation to travel through life. There are distinct types of realms. They can either act in unison to help keep us balanced, or act in conflict with each other adding to upset. Each type of realm has its own goal or benefit. These can overlap. One benefit which most realms have in common is *social interaction*. Our lives pass through several areas where we interact with others on different levels. We also need a *personal realm*. This represents the time to ourselves to regroup, recharge, and refresh. It is also time to reconnect with our spirituality.

Examples of Realms:

- **Personal time** – This constitutes alone time: morning coffee, daily jog, walking the dog, meditation, running errands
- **Home** – House/complex/community, people with whom you live, neighbors, postal carrier, gardener
- **Family** - People beyond those you live with (Home): extended family, in-laws, children who have moved out of the house
- **Friends and Family** – a catch-all realm
- **Work** - co-workers, clients, associates, patrons, suppliers
- **School** - classmates, teachers, study groups, campus organizations/clubs
- **Church** - craft groups, Bible studies, governing boards
- **Sports** - gym, softball/bowling/basketball leagues, cycling, kayaking, hiking groups
- **Recovery** - AA, NA, DA, ACA, Al-Anon, therapy
- **Internet** - Social media, online trading, online shopping, gaming
- **Pub or Dance Hall** - 2 Stepping, billiards, dog park; general social time with friends
- **Medical** - Primary Care Physician, diabetes clinic, dialysis unit, physical therapy

The commonality with realms is the benefits we receive from participating in each one. Individual realms may include multiple benefits. Benefits may overlap from realm to realm. Benefits may also be misleading as an apparent "lack of benefit" to a realm may include a type of secondary gain (such as codependency, which will be explained later).

Benefits from realms may include:

Financial - Sustain the funds for quality of living

Self fulfillment – Accepting yourself in the moment

Challenge – Getting outside your comfort zone to grow physically, emotionally or intellectually

Health/medical - maintain quality of health

Spiritual - connectedness to the universe, God, or bigger picture; serenity

Personal - alone downtime to regroup or heal

Realms appear in the following categories:

- Spiritual
- Social
- Recreational
- Vocational/Educational
- Medical
- Legal
- Personal

Realms can also be divided into 2 distinct categories; the "Have-to's" and the "Want-to's".

"Have-to's" are slices of the pie that are needed, but not necessarily desired. There is usually a reason, a need, for maintaining such a realm. "Have-to's" can often be seen as the *responsible* tasks in our lives. These needs may be approached with caution, trepidation, and stress. Most people do not look forward to going to the dentist for regular periodontal work. Some people feel trapped in a job or career which they feel there is no way out. A relationship may have grown stale, or even abusive, and returning home at the end of the day may be painfully unavoidable.

"Want-to's" are the areas in our lives where we find pleasure, comfort, and security. We usually choose these based on our spiritual beliefs, interests, and ability to distract us from the "Have-to's". "Want-to's" may include weekly ski trips to the mountains, Thursday night line dance lessons, Sunday worship in church, sleeping-in during the weekends, and Friday nights out with friends. The pleasure we gain from experiencing these slices of our life help to maintain our sense of purpose and enjoyment of life. Lack of these slices usually leads to depression, stress, and loss of self.

To create balance, the stress created by the "Have-to's" needs to be balanced out by the "Want-to's". Vacations and weekends may offer a balance to a stressful job. Other positives to add balance to a stressful day are looking forward to spending time with your kids at the end of the day, or a soak in a hot bath or jacuzzi. It is also helpful to know when a "Have-to" is starting to gobble the time of the "Want-to's" that this may be a temporary shift in your balance. Some jobs, seasons, or projects are time-limited. Holding onto a goal and some peace at the end can serve as a nugget to keep us balanced during these periods.

Sub-Realms

Just as a slice of pie could have a layer of meringue or whipped cream, realms can also have smaller areas within the same "slice". Examples may include being on a committee at work, being a member of a community watch program at home or singing in your choir at church. These events/activities may not be necessary and may add or detract from your overall balance and fulfillment.

Manageability of Realms

We lose the balance in our lives when our realms become unmanageable. Undue stress in one realm can tip the balance of all realms, leading to an overall stressed life.

Unmanageability occurs when the "Have-to's" start to devour the "Want-to's", as well as the other way around. We may place the fun and pleasurable things in our life before the responsible tasks, adding upset to the balance and also threatening intimate connections with others.

Manageable realms can turn unmanageable. When this happens slowly, such as in an abusive relationship, we may not take notice until much later when we are at an extreme. An enjoyable job, a volunteer position in the community, or an active role in a sports team may also be roles within realms that slowly evolve into taking more time and effort than originally planned. As one realm grows, others shrink or disappear. Loss of self in a relationship occurs when focus is lost, and we stop tending to factors of intimacy.

Dark Realms

There are 3 distinct types of realms which create and perpetuate imbalance: Codependency, addiction, and boredom. Identifying the presence of these realms is necessary in working to eliminate them and (hopefully) replace them with something healthier.

Dark realms also inhibit personal growth. Dark realms are like cosmic black holes. Black holes in space absorb energy and have a gravitational field that nothing can escape. Light cannot even escape their attraction. Dark realms keep people *stuck* in the same way. They create a dark shadow, and are often accompanied with stress, anxiety, isolation, and depression. It is hard to pull away from the gravity and get out of a dark realm. Falling into one usually happens over a period of time, and with lack of awareness that it is happening. The structure and rituals of these realms, or complete absence of, creates an illusion of hopelessness. Actively working to increase healthier realms is the only way out of this negative cycle.

#1 Codependency

Realms are slices of your life filled with purpose, structure, and individuals. It is not practical nor healthy to have a person "be" an entire slice. It is, however, possible to have a slice that only has one person in it. There is a difference. The *focus* is the key difference. If *non*-dark realms create a sense of purpose, fulfillment, structure, and ritual, then a codependent realm creates this as an illusion while focusing on another. Loss of self results, followed by frustration and unfulfillment.

Codependency is not knowing where you end, and another begins. It involves a dance, or a chase, that only travels in circles. A codependent is a primary enabler, or referee, who is unable to set limits for themself, and who places others' needs before their own.

Codependency is a result of the false self. The false self is created when we learn to deny our own needs and purpose for the sake of holding onto another person. It is a detachment from our own needs and genuine self. We hold on due to fear of loss and abandonment. The secondary gains of codependency are an illusion of security, and an ability to maintain stress at a familiar level.

Codependents might share a common factor of *need*. Intense need results in enmeshment, which is truly a loss of self, as well as a loss of true intimacy. Codependent relationships perpetuate internal dysfunction and prohibit personal growth. It is difficult to achieve true intimacy while trapped in this cycle.

In a codependent relationship, factors of intimacy might be switched, over time, with intimacy killing factors. These negative factors may include abuse, anger, blame, resentment, and conflict. Refer to the list on Appendix V at the end of the book.

#2 Addiction

Addicted behaviors, the lifestyle that accompanies them, and the people who fill this slice create a realm that can grow like a cancerous tumor. Most addictions start out as components to various realms: the beer at the end of a softball game, the gambling during bowling league championship games in Las Vegas, or pain medication following a medical procedure. These activities can be harmless in their infancy. When unchecked, or fueled, they can grow to spill into and cast a shadow over other realms.

Addictions are deceptive, and several think they *need* the substance or ritual to "be normal". This is the illusion that grows from dependency. Denial is another part of the illusion that everything is well. Dependency and denial take their toll on intimacy and the quality of surrounding relationships.

Just as cancer invades healthy cells, addiction can become its own realm, as well as creep into and invade other realms. For example; alcohol might be a part of a "pub" realm; hanging out at the local bar on Friday nights, drinking, and shooting billiards. As drinking increases, it may spill over into the "home slice" and affect relationships and intimacy in that realm. If drinking progresses, a hangover on Monday may affect the "work slice". Work may be missed due to the hangover and recovery, or drinking may continue on the job. Intimacy with family becomes estranged, and "friends" usually turn into "drinking/using buddies". The alcohol in this example can be substituted with marijuana, meth, abused psychotropic medications and pain pills, gambling, sexual compulsions, excessive codependency, excessive cleaning, hoarding, or food.

If unchecked, the drug of choice or addictive behavior can consume each realm in the entire pie. When this drug or behavior reaches the spiritual, True Private level, there is little time, energy, and focus on having any intimacy with others.

#3 Boredom

Boredom is an empty slice. In this slice, a large amount of time is spent without direction or focus.

The boredom slice usually appears when another slice is removed. Our lives are fluid, and we travel through life entering and exiting realms as we go. We may create and enter a high school realm. After 4 years, we graduate and leave this realm behind us. We may then create and enter a realm of college, work, or family. We transition, and our pie slices adapt. If we leave high school and have nothing planned, no "what's next?", and no sense of direction, we may find ourselves drowning in down time. This is the dark realm of boredom. Depression, low self-esteem, and maladaptive behavior follow.

The old adage states, "If you fail to plan, you plan to fail."

Realms need to be tended. An absence in the overall pie needs to be filled with a new realm, or an existing realm needs to expand to cover the absent slice.

Boredom can be lethal if it is replacing a realm of addiction. A person in recovery, theoretically, is moving *out* of "drinking", "drugging", "gambling", "shopping", etc. The transition is normally *into* a new realm of recovery. Unfortunately, the slice of recovery is often not the *same sized slice* as the realm it is replacing. It is smaller. This creates a gap or "boredom" slice created out of the open time remaining. Usually, in time, this slice is filled with something familiar; the return of the addiction.

Social Media, the Gray Realm

Modern technology and social media make it possible to be "friends" with hundreds, if not thousands, of people. Anyone can have a *following* and celebrity status if they choose. Not long ago, people were not as *connected* or *exposed*. Privacy and anonymity were concepts we cherished. We also accepted privacy as a norm.

The amount of time looking into a computer, tablet or smartphone can create an entire realm. We fill our social media with dozens, or even hundreds, of "friends". For those involved in social media, much time and effort go into maintaining an online identity. Because of the relationships, and time/purpose, this becomes its own realm.

Most connections we have through social media are shallow, lacking the contact and exposure to develop several of the factors of intimacy. We may post pictures of our breakfast, our kittens, or our commute to work. We share our political views.

We share our emotions. We share our happy moments, and let the world know when we are having a bad day. We may hook up with a stranger for sex or may enjoy playing online games with people who we have never met in person. The deepest relationship here is the relationship one has with their smartphone or computer.

There is an illusion of intimacy with social media. In the past, people moved away, left college, dropped out of social groups, and were rarely, to never, heard from again. Social media now allows us to remain "friends" with these people. We add "friends" to our lives as we go, but we are no longer "replacing" friendships as people now rarely disappear from our radar. We appear to have more contacts and richer relationships in our lives. This is the illusion. A message, text, or email can be cut and pasted and sent out to several individuals simultaneously. Personalization and time spent for a sincere and unique letter or phone call is lost. We are dealing now with *contact management* versus dealing with true intimacy. In life, when we lose a friend, we usually feel it. In social media, when we are "unfriended", we may never notice the loss.

As our own celebrities, we might use social media to share our misery. Some people use passive aggressive posts when upset, throwing out an indirect communication and hoping others read-between-the-lines. This is a way out and a mean to whine for sympathy. "I am so sick" "I hate my boss" "Pray for me, I am going to the dentist" "I hate Mondays" "I am depressed, and no one cares." Just because we throw our inner dialogue out to the world does not mean the world will stop and take note. If we had true intimacy with our friends, we would know that they also have their own inner dialogue. Personally reaching out to others for help is intimacy; broadcasting for sympathy is not.

More basic media, such as emails and texting, also lacks the depth of communication. The spoken words, along with tone, rate of speech, volume, facial expression, eye contact, posture, and other body language all make up the total package of communication. This is how we communicate a message, and how we communicate how we have received that message. By simply sending text/verbiage, subtle nuances are missing, and the true message can be easily misinterpreted. Unfortunately, we are relying more on electronic interactions and losing contact with others and intimacy in the process.

Overall, what makes this a gray realm, and not dark realm, is that social media does not have to be a bad thing. It may be far too easy to fall into the trap of being linked to your computer or phone, but it doesn't have to be taken to that extreme. In moderation, reading social media may be as relaxing as reading a morning newspaper while sipping a first cup of coffee. Texting can be a means to set up a date or arrange an event to come together and share a real-time experience.

The media of television can also be included in this. It is often referred to as the "drug with a plug." In early days of television, watching weekly shows was a cherished family event. Everyone gathered around the television (and before that radio) as a family unit. It was a special time together, and discussed all week. As television became more mainstream it lost its wonder. With an explosion of available channels, and a TV in every room, families no longer needed to come together or interact. Having a television on during mealtime added to the breakdown of communication and intimacy.

Television is a boredom filler. It has become a comfort food that people turn to when they are stressed. In drug and alcohol recovery, people often transfer their addiction to the couch and television. Streaming access further increased the endless availability of entertainment, and the term *binge watching* was born.

Television can be a slice within the "home slice". It can take time and energy away from other activities that may offer more challenge, pleasure, or intimacy. Households that are void of television usually consist of more daily interaction and a higher level of communication.

Self-Esteem Amongst Realms

Self-esteem is not a simple, all-or-nothing concept. Self-esteem is the culmination of several factors, such as confidence, self-like, competence, or the opposite of these. They are averaged in order of the weight of each factor. These factors are usually tied into individual realms, meaning that you might feel good about yourself in your *work realm*; you may be respected, competent, and at the top of your game. You know this and feel good about this. But in personal relationships, you may have doubt. At *home*, you may feel discouraged in your parenting. You may feel withdrawn from your spouse. Both of these examples can exist at the same time, and one may outweigh the other.

Low self-esteem in one realm may carry into other realms where it is higher, only to infect the other realms. Using the example of high self-esteem at *work* and low self-esteem at *home*, the effects at *home* may lead to poor sleep or depression. In time, this may carry into work and other realms, affecting performance, confidence, manageability, and self-esteem in those realms. Another possible reaction may be to start spending more time at *work*, making this realm bigger and more important, and neglecting the relationships in the *home* realm.

It is important to review and identify the strengths and weaknesses in each realm and see if other realms are affected. If your self-esteem is low because you are on a bowling league and feel bad about your bowling ability, you can either try and improve your skill, or accept your skill. This holds true in other areas and other roles. Maybe at *home*, you are not the best cook or housekeeper. Accepting your skill entails making peace with it and removing judgment.

Healthy self-esteem arises from targeting the specific realms where the low self-esteem exists and working on healing the missing factors of intimacy. It may also include removing intimacy killing factors such as fear and shame. Accepting your overall self-esteem among realms is the key.

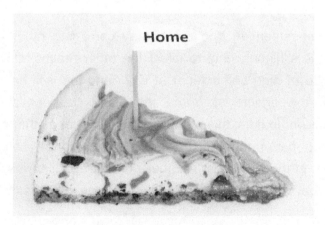

Home

4: Anchors

Anchors are the people in our life who give us a sense of grounding. They represent familiarity and comfort. They give us consistency and feelings of security.

As children, our primary anchors were our parents/primary caregivers. This is the basic and earliest attachment. We derive our sense of wellbeing and security from this attachment. As we grow older, we adopt and incorporate other attachments into our lives; our first grade teacher, our little league coach, or our best friend. After puberty, we gain a new sense of curiosity and explore other areas in life, add new rituals, and hope to gain new attachments along the way. We start a job, we leave home for college, or we start our own family. We move away from what is familiar as we build our own new rituals and structure. In doing so we create new relationships that help keep us directed and grounded. The direction might not always be positive, but it is direction nonetheless.

Often times we are desensitized and oblivious to the people in our life who anchor us. We may be aware of our primary supports, our spouse, our children, or a specific co-worker. But we may lose awareness of other people who are in our outer circles. These people may give our lives consistency and grounding without our awareness. When we get lost in our routine, and structure becomes *normal*, we may lose the value and awareness of how important our anchors are. When they are suddenly gone, we may feel uneasy or unfocused without understanding why. This can be something as simple as stopping at your favorite coffee place in the morning on your way to work and having someone other than your regular server make your coffee. This subtle change in structure and absence from a regular anchor may be enough to shape your day differently than normal. Something is just not quite right but you don't know what it is.

Other things beyond people may anchor us as well. As anchors are tied into ritual and structure, we may also rely on non-human contact to anchor us. Structure is a good thing but being anchored to items and tasks we may do alone limits us from human contact and intimacy. Examples may include:

- Being anchored to the structure of an inflexible workout schedule
- Feeling anchored to the comfort of your bed or home to the point of isolation
- Inability to break out of obsessive behaviors

Being anchored to these non-human things will usually appear in your varied slices on your Intimacy Gram. They will typically show as rather large slices filled with few or no people.

Not all non-human anchors are bad. Taking time once a week to wash your car, enjoying a daily 2 mile run, or finding peace while preparing dinner may be positive rituals that fit into your Personal slice. This structure acts as a positive means of anchoring us. The danger starts if we spend too much time in this realm. Introverts certainly will spend more time here than a socially-charged extrovert. Too much time here creates isolation from others, and decreases the availability of intimate relationships.

5: Initial Charting

Putting it all together: Instructions on how to assemble your Intimacy Gram

The individual pieces of this tool have been outlined and described. For the tool to be effective, some assembly is required. Follow these simple directions. Place tab "A" into slot "A"...

Understanding the concepts is just the beginning. This is a tool that *physically needs to be written down* or crafted on your computer. To get the greatest benefit, you have to do the work, taking note at each step. This intimacy diagram is a visual tool. If you think you can just do it in your head, you will miss the greater understanding of your connections and balance. On paper, this is a detailed visualization of a momentary "snapshot" of your life. This detail cannot be accomplished through self will and assumption. When done thoroughly, people actually find surprises when they put it all down on paper their first time.

People in a recovery fellowship, such as Alcoholics Anonymous, know the importance of fully working the 12 steps. Trying to cut corners by avoiding accountability, and not physically completing the work, stops growth and leads to a lack of recovery. In this sense it is just as important to be accountable and rigorously honest when setting out to draft an Intimacy Gram. The result comes from the work. It is best to set time aside to sit in a quiet place, uninterrupted, and work on your list. If you do it on-the-fly, add to your list via a sticky or a note on your smartphone.

To prepare, all you will need are a few pieces of paper and a pen or pencil. Pencils are preferred as there is usually a lot of erasing and re-doing the first time around. Some choose to take the visual effect to another level and use colored pencils or markers. Know that you can practice drafting your intimacy diagram with scribbles and erase marks, and then rewrite it when the practice draft is completed.

Start with a List: Save for later attachment to your diagram

In preparation for your Intimacy Gram, draft out a list of the people you know. Past or present; it does not matter. Usually, persons who are closest to us are the first ones who come to mind. People with whom we have had recent contact may also appear on this list. Depending on the size of your family, age, and the amount of people who you are in regular contact with, this initial list should have between 50 and 100 people in it. This might sound like a lot, but most people have, in the ballpark, 50 relatives within their extended family.

Take this page and set it aside. If other significant friends, family, coworkers, neighbors, professionals, or associates come to mind, return to the list and add them. It does not have to be a comprehensive list of every person you have known in your entire life.

Create List #2

On another piece of paper, list your different realms. You may have already thought of them as you were thinking of the different areas that came to mind when pulling people for the first list. Some realms might seem to be minor, and others may seem to be smaller portions of a bigger realm (example: your church choir slice may be a part of your bigger church experience, just as sitting on your child's Parent-Teacher Association is a part of the entire school experience).

The list of realms should not be nearly as extensive as the list of people. Most realm lists are generally 4-10 items. When you feel confident with your list, give each "slice" on your list a percentage of how big it is in relation to the entire list. The entire list needs to add up to 100%. If your list falls short of 100%, or goes above it, refigure the percentages to equal 100%. You may be doing this during a time of transition; switching from school to work, going through a divorce, expecting your first child, or preparing for retirement. If this is the case, it may seem difficult to properly add your percentages. This is OK. Realms change. Life is fluid and subject to change. Try to add your realms up as they are in the present. This is a here-and-now snapshot.

The *people list* and the *realm list* are the framework from which you will draw upon to complete your diagram.

Create a Template

On a fresh piece of paper, begin your Intimacy Gram. Start by drawing a circle in the middle of the paper. A nickel could be used as a template for this circle. In the center of this circle, write your name and the current date. Next, draw 4 concentric circles. The first should be about an inch from the original circle, and each one after that should be about an inch from the previous. The end result will look like ripples in a pond. Label the first section away from the center as *True Private*, the next section as *Private*, the next section as *Personal*, the next section as *Familiar*, and the outer section as *Distant*.

Next, *add your pie chart to the rings.* By drawing lines that radiate away from your central circle, divide your pie according to the slices and percentages taken from your *realm list*. When you are finished, your diagram should look something like a bulls-eye or a spider web. *At the outer edge, write the **name** of each slice to **identify the realm**.* Once you are fairly satisfied with your diagram, you are ready to start populating it. (See Appendix I for the Intimacy Gram template)

Put it Together: Insert lists #1 and #2

Refer back to your *people list*. You will now take people from this list and place them in your diagram.

Realm placement: Transfer the names from your list to populate your diagram. Place each person's name in the appropriate slice. List people only once on your diagram.

Some people may be present in more than one realm. Example; you may attend church with your spouse and children. Your spouse may also be part of your hiking/adventure group. If you live with your spouse and children, you would place them in your *home slice*, and you only need to place them once in the diagram. Place each person in the one predominant slice they occupy.

Levels of intimacy placement: Once you identify which realm to place a person into, write their name in the level of closeness that best signifies the intensity of the intimacy. These levels are not absolutes, as some relationships may be placed on the fringes between 2 levels of intimacy. Be honest with yourself and place these people based on the "building blocks" of intimacy you have in their individual "box". *Do not* place them in the level where you would desire them to be.

As you populate the diagram with more names, you may realize a different perspective, and need to do some slight adjusting or rearranging. This is where an eraser may come in handy. It is also alright to start over with a fresh piece of paper. This is part of the learning curve involved as you begin to see the relative differences in relationships and realms.

Initially, most who are completing their first draft place people one ring *inward,* too close, or one ring *outward,* too far.

Another common mistake is focusing more on the factor of *love* and ignoring the others. This is not a diagram to see whom you love. Keep in mind all of the building blocks that contribute to intimacy.

Try not to censor yourself. Some people place therapists and friends closer than they are in reality only out of fear of offending them. If anything, this is open ground for healthy communication.

The Factors of Intimacy Worksheet may be helpful in analyzing and understanding certain key relationships (Appendix V).

Anchors

Next step: draw a circle around the names of the people who serve as your anchors.

Note the people on the diagram who give you a sense of grounding. You may find them in all realms and at all levels. A well-grounded person may have several anchors. If you are an isolator, or have trouble connecting with others, you may have very few identifiable anchors. Ask yourself, "Who are the people who shape my day, and give me a sense of routine or structure?" or "Who would I instinctively call in an emergency?"

Identify these people by placing a circle around their name. If you choose to be creative, use a different colored pen or marker, such as red, to make your circle.

Once the significant names are populated on the diagram, and the anchors are circled, your initial Intimacy Gram charting is complete.

6: Assessment

It's time to unfold the road map and see where you are.

The best person for interpreting your completed Intimacy Gram *is you*. We are all on a different path. How aligned are your relationships, dreams, and goals with what you see on this diagram?

There are usually a few surprises, such as having more people in your life than you previously thought or realizing there are more opportunities for relationships than you are taking. This is the beginning of a heightened sense of self-awareness. The completed tool is brought to a new level when it is discussed with a therapist, life coach, or sponsor.

When analyzing your Intimacy Gram, assess the following concepts:

Realms:
- Balance/Voids
- Dark Realms
- Self-Esteem
- Satisfaction
- Transition

Relationships:
- Placement
- Numbers
- Distribution
- Fulfillment
- Common Deficits (factors)

Anchors
- Identification
- Utilization

First Impressions

What are the most important aspects that you notice when looking at the completed diagram? Usually there are one to two things that stand out the first time an Intimacy Gram is completed. Sometimes, the information is a bit overwhelming.

Looking at your Intimacy Gram, are you satisfied with the life you see?

Satisfaction: this is a big word, and it can be a scary word. Most people are driven to look at their lives because of a certain level of dissatisfaction that they are experiencing. The dissatisfaction might be a result of negative consequences, such a DUI or crumbling marriage. This is the positive thrust for self-help, therapy, and recovery programs. Hopefully, the end goal is to reach a desired level of overall satisfaction. Understanding the dissatisfaction can be a catalyst for change and moving to a more positive and balanced life.

Awareness can be bittersweet. If we see more relationships and opportunities than we thought we had around us, we might feel joy and relief. If we see dark holes in our life we may also feel relief in knowing the cause and knowing there is direction in replacing these holes. Or, we may just feel despair. *Give yourself time and patience to digest and process the information from your initial Intimacy Gram.* Also give yourself support in discussing the diagram with others as you absorb the information.

A negative reaction to your diagram could trigger poor self-esteem. Comparing yourself to an ideal Intimacy Gram, or thinking that your diagram *should* be more balanced, only triggers a shame response. Like a driver's license picture that you do not like, change might not be easy, but it is possible. It just takes time and effort. Going through the correct process may lead to eventual satisfaction. Your map might just be showing you that you have farther to go on your journey to get where you want to be, but *farther* doesn't mean that you can't get there. Positively thinking ahead to an ideal Intimacy Gram may bring the needed hope to make it all possible.

Realms

For analyzing realms, first look to see if they are balanced as ideally as you would like. Life happens and sometimes we forget that we have any control over the life around us. When this happens, we sacrifice activities and associations that are important to us. We may even be living somebody else's pie chart. We all have obligations. Sometimes "have-to's" take over and we forget about the "want-to's".

Look for dark realms. Codependency and addiction are easy to ignore in everyday life, but clearly seeing the space they take up on your diagram can be eye opening. Dark realms are hard to ignore once they are in plain sight.

The ideal pie chart isn't always possible. The question is, realistically, how far off the ideal are you? The ideal might be something that is attainable, but not until months or years into the future. This is where planning comes in. For now, target which slices, if any, are causing stress. Understanding the realm where the stress originates gives a good understanding of how to gain the needed coping skills. If one slice is becoming stressful, and maybe outgrowing its desired size, is there a healthy substitute slice to increase, shrinking or replacing the unhealthy one? Is this a Dark Realm, however small?

We often hold onto realms past their usefulness. We might have outgrown one or are no longer interested in what it holds. If this is the case, it might be easier to replace this with a new realm, or enlarge an existing realm, to bring balance back to your life. Example; if you have volunteered to coach your kids' soccer for the last 5 years and feel a burn out, maybe it might be time to step back and put more time and focus into your stand-up paddle board interest.

Assess the presence of your self-esteem on the diagram. Self-esteem can best be described as your self-confidence *and* your self-like. On a scale of 0 to 5, with 5 being very good self-esteem and 0 being none, rate your self-esteem within each realm. Each realm offers its own unique social situations, challenges, and needed skills (social, technical, or physical). How you feel about yourself in each realm may vary. Write your score at the outer edge of each slice on your diagram.

Transitions

Life is change. Maintaining balance can be as tricky as a lumberjack trying to stand on a log floating in the water. Currents change, and balance must be shifted. We transition from realm to realm during milestones in our lives: graduation from college, marriage, the birth of our first child, change in job, and retirement. Often times, these are planned, and we can take time to design our future realms and how we can transition into them.

Transition can also be sudden and difficult. Life can throw us a curveball: sudden death in the family, loss of mobility, victim of a violent crime or car accident, and loss of work, just to name a few traumas. Entering recovery from addiction is also a huge transition. These transitions are characterized by leaving a comfort zone and moving into unknown and unfamiliar realms. It is also a transition in your identity and culture (moving from a using culture to a sober one). This transition is often characterized by grief and loss. Loss might require "letting go". Most fail at recovery from addiction by reverting to old and familiar realms. This is how failure in letting go of an old, dysfunctional identity leads to perpetuation of old cycles, as well as ongoing pain.

The Intimacy Gram is a tool to help chart transition and shift in realms. This is the GPS/road map aspect of the tool that helps you plan direction.

Relationships

When analyzing relationships, it is best to try and answer the following questions:

- Do I have too many relationships, spreading myself too thin?
- Am I lacking relationships in my inner circles?
- Do my relationships lift me up or pull me down?
- Are my relationships based on intimacy, or dark realm behaviors?
- Are my key relationships connected with each other, or do I keep them compartmentalized in their own realms?

Due to transportation, media, and the abundance of social options in most communities, we have more relationships as a society today than we have had in history. With this abundance around us, and the demand of society to keep connected, it is very easy to spread ourselves too thin. We do this when we find most relationships in our outer circles, and a detachment from those who should be in our inner ones.

For specific relationships:

- Are people where you want them on your diagram?
- Do you have the desired closeness?
- Are relationships kept at a distance, holding yourself back due to hurt, lack of skills, or lack of self-esteem?
- Are you able to identify the missing factors of intimacy that you can possibly work on building?
- Do you see a theme of missing factors that are common to all your relationships?

If there is a pattern, it is usually because the factors of intimacy are learned. We may *not* have learned how to be proficient with all the factors. Working to strengthen the missing or weak factors might be best when surrounding yourself with others who have these traits, or interacting with a therapist or sponsor. We might also gravitate towards others who exemplify traits we lack in hopes of a complementary relationship.

7: Planning/Action

Every journey begins with an idea. The idea becomes a plan and the plan is put into action. Change only happens when we set ourselves into *action*., moving to do the necessary work. The completed Intimacy Gram offers insight. It is up to *you* to determine the direction and actions you wish to take in improving relationships and adding more balance to your life.

Balancing Realms

If your pie chart is not balanced, what would your realistic ideal be, and what steps do you need to take to make this a reality? Action steps might include creating temporary realms (to help you achieve short term goals). These will lead to more permanent realms (that fulfill long term goals). An example of this might be to have a desire to replace your work slice with a

86

new job or career but needing to create a temporary school slice to help you achieve this goal. It is important to understand the short term goals which lead to your long term goals; short term goals are action steps in achieving change.

Be aware that when you add to the energy and size of one realm, you are taking away from another. Stress often happens when we try to add too much to the pie, only to find out it will not all fit. It is usually best to focus on changing one realm at a time and working on the adjustment of others as may be necessary.

We often feel unbalanced when we are transitioning from one realm to another. If we feel uncomfortable we might rely on a dark realm to give us comfort, or an illusion of security. In understanding the *process* of transition, we are better able to cope and maintain balance through this process. Pace yourself.

Self-Esteem

Are you comfortable with the scores you assessed, or would you like to build a greater sense of self-confidence and self-like among your realms? Improvement with self-esteem should result from the work done to improve your factors of intimacy and finding balance in your realms. Improvement also comes from developing a positive relationship with your higher power. Continued work in this area can be with a therapist, sponsor, minister, or life coach.

Strengthening the Quality of your Relationships

The best way to ensure the quality relationships, and build new positive relationships, is to focus on the factors of intimacy.

In reviewing the patterns in your relationships, you probably have already found that there are certain key factors that you struggle with. It is often helpful if you can choose one or two of the factors and focus on practicing the targeted factors in effort to strengthen them.

Sometimes we are lacking factors we were never taught. In this case, a therapist, life coach, pastor, or friend might help in modeling and teaching the desired traits. When looking at relationships we wish to strengthen or move from an outer circle to an inner circle, choose people who model these attributes. Choose the people who will lift you up and have the factors of intimacy you wish to have yourself.

Target the specific relationships which need tending to by drawing an arrow on your Intimacy Gram from the name of the person you are targeting and aim the arrow inward towards the next inner level of intimacy. This is like adding a routing direction to your road map.

Anchors

When we understand the significance of our anchors, we have new choices for maintaining and improving balance. This awareness is something that stands out, and you can't unsee it once it is there. It is like buying a new model car that you are not familiar with; once you have it, you start noticing this model everywhere. By realizing the *significance* of our anchors, we can thus see new opportunities, and choose to expand upon or embellish these relationships.

Often times we have people around us, in our outer levels, who have the potential to be great friends. Our own deficits of intimacy and need to attract unhealthy people prevent us from realizing the quality of those positive people who we have around us. Realizing this, an anchor in one of your outer levels of intimacy may be somebody to target for bringing in closer to your inner circles.

Healthy Detachment

While we may need to fill our inner circles (Personal and

Private levels of intimacy), we may also need to move some people into our outer circles (Familiar and Distant levels of intimacy).

Placing appropriate boundaries and distance from friends, family, and associates is a tricky task. It tends to be easiest when omitting a dark realm and those who are included in it. For example, if you give up drinking, you will likely give up going into the local bar with friends. The bar goes away with the alcohol, as do the associates inside the bar. It becomes difficult when you remove the "bar realm" yet have friends and family who drink within your other realms. It is not always necessary or practical to remove these people from your life, but healthy balance is maintained when boundaries are put in place to better define the relationships. Respect, support, acceptance, and communication are a few factors at play here.

Creating and maintaining new realms, or strengthening healthy relationships, aids the process of detachment.

Detachment becomes overwhelming when you are first trying to remove yourself from a negative or dysfunctional culture (drinking culture, critical culture, abusive culture, etc.). Adding a realm of a 12-Step Fellowship or other support group is helpful when extra support is needed during transition between cultures.

8: Ghost Relationships

Ghost Relationships are the past relationships that overshadow present ones. Oftentimes, these are people from the past who were abusive, critical, and negatively influential in our development. Some think of these as the skeletons in the closet. They could be deceased, estranged, or still present in everyday life.

You may find yourself reacting harshly to your boss, or having difficulty connecting with your spouse. The truth is, your reactions might not be in defense against these people, but rather against ghosts from the past who you are projecting onto these people. A disdain for authority might be an ongoing reaction based in a defense against an extremely controlling parent or caregiver. Reacting against a projection of a past relationship that you may be placing on a current relationship creates a wall. This wall voids the factors of intimacy and is an intimacy-killer.

Ghost relationships may also be different incarnations of people who are still in our lives today. We may have been raised by parents who were emotionally unstable, abusive, rigid, or were chemically dependent. As we have grown older, they may have gone through treatment and recovery, no longer being emotionally unavailable. Our present relationships may be good with these people, yet the old incarnations still may cast a shadow in our present. We developed coping and defense reactions to these people in our childhood, and still may be triggered to react against projections of authority today. We are reacting through a *past perspective*. This can be deceiving because we may think we have worked through past pain. "I have a great relationship with my parent today." This is how we function as adults, and we often fail to see the hurt inner child within us who reacts when facing threat of past pain or rejection.

Past perspectives are based in the memories we hold, and the point-of-view in which we recorded the memories. If you have ever returned to an old childhood home, only to be surprised at how much smaller the rooms seem to be, it is because you recorded the memory when you were of a smaller size and the room was much bigger to you.

From our young, vulnerable states we may remember authority figures to be very powerful, scary, threatening, and abusive. As we were powerless in our childhood, emotions like fear and vulnerability are linked to these memories. Oftentimes, we have buried these memories to a place where we are not conscious of them. They are still there, and we react in the presence of someone who somehow reminds us of our earlier abusers or criticizers. This is actually the root of most of our insecurities and resentments, and we play them out again and again.

An advanced assessment of your Intimacy Gram includes looking at present people who are in your circles today, and identifying the "ghost relationships" you may be projecting onto these people. This could include an identification that you react to your wife as you used to react to your mother, or that you react to your boss (and usually most authority figures) as you reacted to your father or grandfather. This identification usually comes after examining the patterns of how you interact, and react, to these people, as well as the *resulting emotions*. Understanding the patterns is crucial in working on healing the past trauma and separating the ghost relationship from the present relationship.

Working with a therapist, as well as working a supportive program like Adult Child of Alcoholics (ACA or ACoA) might help in the acceleration of this healing. Share the Intimacy Gram with your sponsor or therapist. Charting subtle changes in the relationships within the diagram could help you to visually see the growth in healing. The goal here is to remove the ghost relationships from present relationships, in order to be fully in the moment. Once you are grounded in the here-and-now, you will be more successful at building factors of intimacy in your current relationships.

9: Hats and Masks

Hats are roles which are true to ourselves and serve a purpose. Masks are the roles which are not genuine to us, and we use these to hide our true selves from others.

The roles we play in any given situation or realm are determined by our personal boundaries. Originally, our boundaries are developed and shaped by others. This happens in formative, childhood years. Later in life a second shift in roles emerges when we attempt to conform and adapt to the expectations that society and others place upon us.

Roles can also be in response to cultural expectations. As children, we are "blank screens" and are taught cultural "norms". This includes both the culture of your community/society, and the culture within your household.

These roles might not feel comfortable later in life as we learn cultural differences and norms outside of our original programming. Many struggle to adapt to these differences, and compensate by taking on various hats and masks.

Hats are the different, yet genuine, roles that we take on in each realm. At work, we may be in the role of team player. At home, we may be in a role of leadership and authority. Working with a trainer at the gym, you may be in the role of student. We might spend a good part of our lives building and defining our roles. Hopefully, we take the boundaries and confidence of each role with us as we discard one realm and transition into a new one. In later years, successful juggling of hats and roles will lead to wisdom, peace, and satisfaction with self.

Masks are the roles we wear that are not congruent with our true selves. They serve as a means of protection. They create a wall based on fear and lack of trust. Walls are protective boundaries that serve as a fortified castle guarding an inner palace. It is difficult to develop deep intimacy with others when you are attempting to connect in a relationship while wearing a mask. The defensive boundaries only let intimacy get to a certain point before it can go no further.

Usually there is often more freedom of choice with the hats we wear versus the masks we hold onto so dearly.

The most common mask is that of *people pleaser*. This mask is usually first worn in childhood following an incident of abandonment or trauma: parents divorced, change in school with loss of friends, or Mom or Dad being emotionally unavailable due to substance use, mental illness, or lack of nurturing and support. This mask goes up to show a care-taking self. "If I take care of you, you will not leave me." This mask stays up due to an element of fear, and while it may protect the individual from abandonment, it also traps the person from gaining a genuine reciprocal relationship.

Note that it may be difficult to identify people-pleasing/excessive caretaking as a mask rather than a role. This mask becomes an integral part of the wearer's identity. There is a risk of fear in looking under this mask. This is based on a belief that without this mask there is zero identity. This can also be true for people wearing a "victim mask". Wearing a victim mask is very different than being victimized or coping with trauma. A victim mask is when a person's entire identity is based on being the underdog and using this as a means to attract sympathy from others. It is a circular, self-sabotaging, pattern that enforces the inability to trust others. It is extremely difficult to shed a victim identity. This is a slow process, and to be successful, this can take years of personal development or therapy.

Other protective masks may serve purposes of keeping us on the defensive, controlling others and situations. This is self-defeating as the hardest things to control are other people, places things, and situations.

The fearful child underneath the mask becomes buried, hidden, and lost. The adult wearing the mask is often unhappy and unfulfilled. Mask-wearers travel from realm to realm, keeping most people in their outer rings of intimacy. Basically, this mask creates a deficit in the factors of intimacy, affecting all relationships in all realms.

When reviewing your completed Intimacy Gram, be sure to examine the various hats you wear in each realm, as well as any potential masks. Masks can be common in the "have-to" realms of our life. If you find masks, you will need to explore what you are hiding, and who you placed the mask up to hide from. Removing masks will build both self-esteem and capacity for intimacy.

10: Maintenance

You have done the draft, you have gained the awareness, and you have done the work. Now the road ahead is about keeping balance and quality. Stay on the course. To avoid getting lost, revise your diagram every 3 months for the first year, and then every six months thereafter. After a while, the concepts will be integrated into your everyday thinking. You will internalize these concepts and be more aware of stressors affecting your balance. The new mindfulness element pertaining to the factors of intimacy and realm balance will help you remain stable and fulfilled.

Waiting until stress appears or relationships begin to fail is putting the review off too long. Preventive maintenance is always far easier than repair and damage control.

Chart Your Progress

Improving and maintaining balance is achieved by working on the following basic goals:

- Enforcing quality of relationships (working at managing crucial factors of intimacy)
- Continued detachment from relationships that deter or distract
- Balancing realms to maintain a healthy homeostasis; realm strengthening and new realm building.
- Removal of unwanted masks.
- Removal of unwanted ghost relationships.

If you find yourself another state of transition, focus on building new realms and strengthening the existing realms that you are keeping. Give this specific focus. Make sure that you are putting the correct amount of time and energy into this; be careful not to sacrifice time from other quality realms, or too little energy to sufficiently grow the realm. Populating the realms will follow.

If you are working on maintaining relationship stability, choose 1-2 specific factors of intimacy to focus on improving. Practice rotating factors from week to week. Being conscious of these specific factors will help you to keep them forefront in your mind. Be creative: place note cards or sticky notes on your refrigerator or desk with the single word factor of the week. As you do this, notice the difference in how others respond to you.

Others will generally reflect positively to your efforts and changes with intimacy. Sometimes, though, people will have difficulty accepting or trusting your efforts. We are all connected, and any changes you make in yourself might alter the tempo of the *dance* between you and another. Not everyone will accept and support your positive changes. Keep the focus on yourself. You can't be responsible for working another person's Intimacy Gram.

Ken Francis, MS

The Intimacy Gram and the 12 Steps

The Intimacy Gram is a perfect tool when working a 12 Step program. Which program, or fellowship, does not matter. The foundation for the steps is the same. The all entail the quest for serenity and a spiritual awakening. The Intimacy Gram parallels the steps and can help bring the work of each step to a deeper level. The Intimacy Gram also helps the sponsor to guide the sponsee. Most people entering recovery have realms that are out of balance, dark realms, and relationships that are lacking in several factors of intimacy. Completing an initial Intimacy Gram prior to starting step work can provide a source of information to draw upon when working the steps. The Intimacy Gram and the fellowship's basic text are two complementary tools which work together to excel the recovery process.

In-depth step work using your Intimacy Gram will also help you explore and identify triggers. We tend to revert to dark-realm behaviors and lose intimacy when situations arise that trigger old defenses and ineffective coping skills. The creation of boredom, which often happens during this transition, can be easily identified and replaced by simple charting on your diagram.

Step 1: *We admitted that we were powerless over (dark realm) - that our lives have become unmanageable.*

Realms are made of people, places, and things. A completed Intimacy Gram can easily diagram unmanageable realms and unmanageable relationships. Sometimes, unmanageability can be easily spotted with the identification of dark realms. Poor boundaries and powerlessness in other realms usually accompany the dark realms and spill over from them.

The resulting powerlessness is from the perpetuation of the tension, stress, and consequences of the unmanageable realms and relationships. It is important to see the self-defeating cycles of rituals and personal interactions in these realms. Some refer to this as the *insanity of the disease.* It is truly a vicious cycle that seems to have no end.

The completed Intimacy Gram gives a valuable list of the

people and realms which hold power over us.

Out of the unmanageability of these dark realms may come new realms. These are *unwanted* "have-to" realms, such as court, DUI classes, a second job to cover extra financial concerns, or medical/health management. Identifying the extra burdens that these added realms place in the overall pie is key in addressing the unmanageability of the original dark realm.

It is also important to identify people who were or "should be" in your inner circles and are not. These relationships have been neglected or damaged and pushed toward the lower levels of intimacy. Loss of trust with these people is most likely a common theme.

Step 2: *Came to believe that a Power greater than ourselves could restore us to sanity.*

The goal here is to examine what is in True Private level of intimacy and prepare to clean house. Spirituality is generally askew at the onset of recovery. We usually have lost our connection with a meaningful Higher Power and have replaced it with an easier and less meaningful one. In the process, we have lost our sincere connections with others.

Look at your Realms and Relationships and identify the

existing insanity. It is usually fairly obvious when looking at the diagram as a whole. What spiritual connection have you lost in this insanity? What should be in your inner, spiritual circles, that is missing? Can you identify your God or Higher Power?

To see yourself as part of a bigger picture, and to define your place in each realm, it is often helpful to make a gratitude list. The list should include the relationships, opportunities, and challenges that you have in each realm. This is how we begin to reconnect with the universe around us.

It is important here to identify your Higher Power and a bigger picture. In the beginning of recovery, your definition may be vague, and your connection might be weak. But this is where you start. Identifying these concepts bring us a sense of connection and hope. If you are drowning, what is the lifeboat that you need to swim to for survival?

Step 3: *Made a decision to turn our will and our lives over to the care of God as we understood God.*

This is the step about entering humility. This is more than seeing yourself as part of a bigger picture, but rather *seeing yourself connected to something greater than yourself*. This is also about letting go of self-will and pride, and working towards the acceptance of the guidance and solutions presented before you. In essence, this is about letting go of undue control over people, places, things, and situations.

In recovery, your drug of choice/behavior of choice, and yourself, can no longer be your Higher Power. We often resist guidance and try to do things on our own. This is like being lost in a forest. You may have a map to help you through the forest, but all paths and trees look the same. As you struggle to get out of the forest, there may be a helicopter above you. The pilot is a "higher power" as he or she has a viewpoint higher than your own, and a clearer ability to see the forest through the trees. *Let them guide you out.* In Step 2 you worked on identifying your Higher Power, and for this step, you will need to work on turning your will over to it.

Surrender and trust are 2 factors of intimacy at play here. If you struggle with trust, or if it is a foreign concept for you, you will no doubt have difficulty with surrendering. It is best to take time and work on lowering walls, reducing self-will, and building trust rather than rushing through this step. Exploring your early messages about trust, and working through them, will be a good segue into Step 4.

Trust and surrender can be huge concepts to grasp and execute. This is not a step to be rushed. To simply say, "I trust God or a Higher Power" is not enough to free your hurt and burden of self-will and control. This needs to be a complete surrender. Compromise in recovery is a set-up for failure because it keeps self-will (run riot) in command. Repeated trials and practice at surrender and trusting others are important as this is more of a transition than it is a simple decision.

What negative realms or relationships are you holding onto that might be keeping your Higher Power from moving into your inner circles of intimacy?

Step 4: *Made a searching and fearless moral inventory of ourselves.*

After looking into accepting our insanity and turning it over, it is time to start examining the crud that we have been carrying around. Depending on how detailed you wish to go, you can put together different Intimacy Grams representing different periods of your life. Like putting together a photo album, you can draft from memory or use drafted diagrams of past years. Yearly Intimacy Grams dating back to childhood give a wealth of information when looking for resentments, trauma, and misunderstandings.

It is also important to visit past realms when putting together your inventory. Past realms include the neighborhood where you grew up, high school and potentially college, past jobs, former churches, sports teams, and social groups. Simply identify each past realm and list the relationships within each realm. Memory recall often improves when you start drafting out the realms and relationships from your past.

Instead of looking at the factors of intimacy that existed in our lives, for the 4th Step, we look at the absence of such factors, as well as the existence of *intimacy-killing factors*. The factors which work against intimacy include:

- Anger
- Avoidance
- Abuse (physical, sexual, verbal, neglect)
- Blame
- Catastrophizing
- Competition
- Conflict
- Conflict of interest
- Depression
- Discontentment
- Dishonesty
- Disinterest
- Disloyalty
- Distrust
- Envy
- Fear

- Greed
- Hate
- Impatience
- Infidelity
- Irrational thinking
- Irresponsibility
- Lust
- Martyrdom
- Mindreading
- Misrepresentation
- Rationalization
- Resentment
- Selfishness
- Shame
- Smothering (excessive caretaking)
- Vengeance
- Unavailability

It is important to identify and include these in our past inventories. As you explore these traits, you may see that there have been patterns in your life where these factors continually arose. Work to trace the root cause, or initial trauma, which started these patterns. If these are present today, you might be able to understand their origins, their triggers, and the irrationalities of holding on to such emotions and behaviors.

Look to identify *ghost relationships* that are attached to the intimacy-killers. These ghost relationships usually have negative emotions, or "bad feelings", attached to them. A major feeling identified and explored in Step 4 is resentment. Resentments are feelings of unresolved anger that you burden yourself with. These feelings are usually underlying your core, and drive you subconsciously. With identification of the primary ghost relationships, you will be able to begin work on healing and letting go.

It is important to stay away from blame when identifying these hurts and ghosts. The goal here is to identify and accept. The ACA Big Read Book states, "Name it, don't blame it." Further healing comes in the later steps.

Step 5: *Admitted to God, to ourselves, and to another human being the exact nature of our wrongs.*

Before doing your 5th Step, review your relationship with your Higher Power. If you are still struggling to build a strong connection to your spirituality, this might not be a good time to complete this step. It is important to have trust in your Higher Power or God before putting this trust in a fellow brother or sister.

The 5th Step is another exercise in trust. It involves purging the junk, hurts and resentments in a forum that is safe and secure. To feel comfortable sharing your 4th Step with your sponsor, review your *factors of intimacy* which you hold with your sponsor. Which building bricks do you have in your sponsor's box? Factors of trust, security, surrender, humility, and vulnerability need to be present to fully share a 4th Step and not feel *damaged* in the process.

Step 6: *Were entirely ready to have God remove all these defects of character.*

This step involves analyzing and identifying difficulty with any of the factors of intimacy. In formative years, we often replace missing factors of intimacy with perceived factors. These turn into character defects (AA) or survival traits (ACA). While these traits may have helped us survive as children, they work against us as intimacy-killers in our adulthood. These defects of character are usually related to the intimacy-killing factors reviewed in Step 4. The actions and behaviors resulting from these feelings usually begin as reaction to pain, trauma, or abandonment. They are the basis of our survival skills. At one point they served an important purpose; to protect us from physical or emotional harm. We might have learned these from others, being the basis of our culture. They unfortunately work against us when we carry these behaviors, defenses, and reactions into our adult lives.

Character defects/survival traits are easily spotted by identifying the masks that we wear. These masks are either worn to keep people very close to us or as a buffer to keep people away. They are ingrained into who we are. We are often aware of these traits and carry them with a sense of powerlessness and shame. Healing comes when we can identify the origins of these defenses.

These defenses are usually attached to *ghost relationships*. This is a reaction to protecting yourself from an original, childhood wound. The defenses probably served as a shield at one time, but are no longer effective or necessary.

Character defects can also be the adoption of a critical parent's voice that now resides in your head but sounds like your own voice instead. Learning self-love and forgiveness for carrying these protective behaviors will bring a new mindfulness to the present, and further healing. Seeing a ghost for what it is, a figment from the past, removes its power. Without the ghost to fight, the protective character defects/survival traits will start to fade away. It is easier to stay mindful in the present when ghosts have been tamed and placed in the past where they belong.

Step 7: *Humbly asked God to remove our shortcomings.*

Here we accept our defects/survival traits and ask for guidance in growth in these areas, looking back to our process (whether it be therapy, 12 steps, or spiritual path) and giving in to follow that process in the here and now. We do this by living in our present Intimacy Gram.

This step also involves a deeper level of surrender. Here you work at letting go of your *failure identity* and giving it to your Higher Power. This is another release of old pain as you work on forgiving yourself and letting go of critical voices in your head.

Be kind and gentle with yourself without the judgment left over from critical ghost relationships.

Step 8: *Made a list of all persons we had harmed, and became willing to make amends to them all.*

Here, we willingly start taking responsibility for our actions without blaming others. Referring to the past Intimacy Grams which you completed for Step 4 will give you a huge resource for Step 8. Use these past diagrams to help identify the relationships where you may have directly or indirectly caused hurt in others.

Hurt is usually caused by the intimacy killing factors, as well as from pulling back on the factors of intimacy. This may reveal itself from past relationships as not trusting, loving, communicating, or compromising enough. Look for relationships where you resisted intimacy and dismissed the factors others were trying to share with you.

Making amends may also be in order for not paying attention to a loss of intimacy. We may be distracted by events or realms that pull us away from important relationships. Often these are the dark realms of addiction and all that goes with it. *Willingness* to make amends is a part of the healing process where we work on changing our behaviors and taking more responsibility for our capacity for intimacy.

Step 9: *Made direct amends to such people wherever possible, except when to do so would injure them or others.*

This is another Step where you put the *factors of intimacy* into action. Balance and self-esteem will increase by admitting accountability to others. Making amends, directly or indirectly, serves as a means of letting go and adopting a new direction. This may include letting go of unfinished business in specific relationships, or strengthening relationships through adding factors of humility and transparency.

Step 10: *Continued to take personal inventory and, when we were wrong, promptly admitted it.*

The steps from Step 10 through Step 12 parallel the maintenance phase of the Intimacy Gram. This requires review of key relationships for their status in Private, Personal, and Familiar levels and working to maintain or improve key factors in those relationships. Tending to these relationships keeps them strong and helps to keep you in balance. Promptly admitting and correcting deficits/factors, such as lack of communication and affection, is a part of the maintenance process.

By focusing on our own factors of intimacy and self-care with balance of realms, we place *Principles* before *Personalities*.

Step 11: *Sought through prayer and meditation to improve our conscious contact with God as we understood God, praying only for knowledge of God's will for us and the power to carry that out.*

Here we return back to gratitude, trying not to live in past or future Intimacy Grams, but living in the present. Prayer and meditation are the basis of mindfulness, our connection with the *moment*. The primary focus here is concentrating on maintaining and strengthening the factors of intimacy with your spiritual and closest relationship. By staying in the present, we are more available to work at maintaining the close relationships that populate our inner circles, as well as with our Higher Power.

Step 12: *Having had a spiritual awakening as the result of these steps, we tried to carry this message to other addicts, and to practice these principles in all our affairs.*

The journey does not end in Step 12. It merely continues. We share this format with others through step work, as well as through personal testimony of experience, strength, hope, and growth in intimacy and recovery. We can also share the principles of the Intimacy Gram with family and friends, even if they aren't in addiction or belong to a 12 Step fellowship. Sharing these principles helps you to be more fully conscious of them. To help keep your spirit awake, you share this process with others. Continue to enhance and strengthen the relationships around you, as well as your relationship with your Higher Power.

The Intimacy Gram and Individual Therapy

An Intimacy Gram can assist in psychotherapy the same way that an Intimacy Gram helps a sponsor walk someone through the 12 Steps. It provides structure to the therapy session, and helps to increase communication, trust, and vulnerability with the client/counselor relationship. It also gives the client the framework and direction to work on issues between therapy sessions.

Therapy can begin or end with any of the 10 components of the Intimacy Gram. Some of us are driven into therapy because of lacking factors of intimacy, while others may have ghost relationships overshadowing their present ones. A client may have quality relationships but lack challenges in realms which have grown stale. Other clients may lack factors of intimacy in addition to lacking coping skills to help them in creating meaningful and balanced realms. Some might be stuck in a transition between realms. Any deficits to the 10 components can be incorporated into a treatment plan. A concrete aspect to this is that it may create a list which patients can work to complete. As tasks and challenges are reached, necessary steps can be made to maintain these gains while moving to the next challenge on the list.

Before actual diagramming of an Intimacy Gram, the concepts of intimacy and balance need to be explored. A certain lack of these elements is typically what brings people into therapy, and it is important to ascertain the patient's understanding of these concepts before moving ahead. Education of the factors might be necessary before charting process. The time spent educating needs to be paced with the client's/patient's ability to comprehend and digest the information. This education process could take weeks, if not months, before starting the initial diagram charting.

Therapists gain additional insight into a client when presented with a completed diagram. The information represented on one piece of paper may save several sessions of exploration. Because there are no hidden secrets in trying to read a completed Intimacy Gram, a therapist needs no special training.

Reviewing the Intimacy Gram creates a partnership between the client and the therapist. This partnership is characterized by an ongoing dialog and shared terminology. The terms, "factors", "realms", "inner circles", and "ghosts" become solid pillars in therapy. These are terms easily remembered by clients during the times between therapy sessions. Simple assignments in therapy might be to work on defining or strengthening realms, identifying ghost relationships which undermine current relationships, and identifying relationships to bring people closer into the inner circles.

Another way the Intimacy Gram can be helpful in therapy is in the development of the therapeutic alliance. The partnership is just one factor of the therapeutic relationship. This relationship is based on several of the factors of intimacy: trust, transparency, genuineness, and compassion, to name a few. If a client shows difficulty in connecting with the therapist, the list of factors can be reviewed and discussed. Building the trust and security of a therapeutic relationship is paramount to success and outcome of therapy.

It is helpful if the therapist has experienced the charting process of their own Intimacy Gram.

Ken Francis, MS

The Intimacy Gram and Group Therapy

The concept of intimacy can expand into something more immersive when processed by a group of people. In addition to increased input, there is also an opportunity within the group to practice some of the basic factors of intimacy.

An effective and interactive way for therapists, life coaches, and sponsors to teach several people the Intimacy Gram is to do so in a psycho-educational group format. Involve class participants by asking them to help create the list of the factors of intimacy. Defining the factors and levels of intimacy, followed by the concept of realms, and then integrating these concepts, is a very concrete way to help a group conceptualize members' own potpourri of intimacy and balance.

A barebones presentation can last anywhere between 60-90 minutes. The core of the diagram includes the first 4 concepts: factors of intimacy, levels of intimacy, realms, and anchors. While this can be taught in a 60-minute format, it is a lot of information for anyone to absorb and digest. Splitting the presentation into two presentations allows for more understanding and retention. The first week would include the factors and the levels. Week two includes realms, diagramming, and identification of anchors on the diagram.

An advanced group can take on a weekly journey through the factors of intimacy, each session discussing a different factor. Processing the Intimacy Gram at a slow pace allows group members the ability to focus on specific factors and take the time to process and digest each.

Groups can be structured to show weekly progress, change, and transition. One example would be to have each member present their current pie chart or simple diagram on a dry erase board. The group members can examine stressors and discuss options/barriers for balance. This allows group input and discussion from all. This can be especially useful in a drug or alcohol recovery group. Relapse signs can often be seen and identified when realms begin to shift or become unbalanced, or when relationships become stressed. Working to re-balance the realms and de-stress relationships may prevent a relapse.

Members who avoid the warning signs and relapse need to review their realms in group immediately following a relapse. Hindsight is 50/50, but review of events leading to off balanced realms and relationships leads to insight of unseen triggers as well new direction. It may also unveil stubbornness to see disastrous shifts as they are happening. This relapse-timeline, alongside of an Intimacy Gram review, works well in group settings. It helps all participants see the hidden relapse processes. Understanding this might lead to increased self-awareness and self-care, and hopefully continued recovery as a result.

Another way the Intimacy Gram can be integrated into group therapy would be to start off each group session with a group "check-in" "go-around". The check-in is a scripted introduction where members chose to introduce themselves with simple statements which can be explored later in the group session. A go-around is simply any exercise where all members in the group circle participate, one at a time. These statements are from options in the script. Examples include "open" or "shut", "factor" or realm", "struggling" or "secure" and "who anchored you today?" This exercise helps ground members in the group journey towards intimacy and opens the group to much discussion (see Appendix IV).

Intimacy Gram Group Check-in:

What did you do well today?
Who anchored you today?
Attached or avoidant?
Honest or dishonest?
Accepting or critical?
Team player or rebellious?
Forgiving or resentful?
Selfish or selfless?
Indulge or restrain?
Abusive or compassionate?
Patient or impatient?
Realm or factor?
Struggling or secure?
What factor/realm can you improve upon?

"Attached or avoidant?" plays on one's willingness and trust levels. A simpler form might be "Open or shut?". This shows where someone currently is in their trust process; how guarded they may be or how defended they may be against vulnerability. Some would consider this exercise an ice-breaker.

The Intimacy Gram and Couples

Sharing two completed Intimacy Grams may be a tool to help open or increase communication in a couple. Whether dueling or complementary, review of a couple's diagrams may help to assess the quality of the relationship, factors which may be missing, and incongruities in balance. Fairly healthy couples can compare and assess their own pair of diagrams. Others may wish to seek the help of a therapist, pastor, or life coach.

Individuals should review their own Intimacy Gram before comparing with their partner. Original focus needs to be on a person's own Intimacy Gram before looking at how it may overlap with another's. Otherwise, the trap is to be more concerned about somebody else's balance and relationships rather than focusing on their own.

As a couple, they should be fairly high-functioning in their relationship before sitting down to review and compare the two diagrams. The goal here is to take a fairly well working relationship and make it better. A certain level of confidence and maturity is needed to process inconsistencies and deficits. Couples with chaos, blaming, distrust, and poor coping skills should not compare Intimacy Grams. This should be placed aside for a time after the couple can work as individuals on balancing their own diagrams separately, and increase the trust and collaboration between themselves.

Maturity is also needed to have an ability for acceptance. Couples might have expectations for their diagram to mirror their partner's. The end goal is to have a diagram that complements more than it mirrors. Unfortunately, some couples have drifted apart, and their diagrams are vastly different. A person may not have placed their partner at the same level of intimacy as their partner has placed them. This is very hurtful to see. Although not surprising as this rift between the two is most likely what brought them into therapy to begin with.

When reviewing Intimacy Grams as a couple, there does not have to be an exact parallel in factors. The key is to look for, or attain, reciprocity in factors. It is not unusual to seek out a partner that has a strong factor for intimacy you may be lacking. This is an example that "opposites attract". Over time, one partner might learn their lacking factors from their partner and adopt these factors into their own.

Realms between a couple's diagrams do not need to be sliced equally, nor should they be mirror images of each other. The key is in each partner mutually finding the right number of shared realms with the other. This varies from couple to couple and relationship to relationship. For example; some couples work together from home or work in the same establishment and find balance by having separate hobbies. Other couples with these conditions find stress and more of a need for time apart. Assessment must be a partnership; what works and what doesn't?

Problems arise when factors and realms are not aligned or complementary. Realms may have too much or too little overlap. One person may place more need, or dependence, on the other person, then be envious or upset if the other person has more balance and better-defined realms. Important factors of intimacy may be missing or barely present. A therapist, pastor, or life coach may assist the couple work together to develop complementary balance in each other's pie. Couples also work at communicating their needs for improving factors where there may be a deficit.

The Intimacy Gram with Internal Family Systems Therapy and The Loving Parent Guidebook

Just as a completed Intimacy Gram makes a reference resource for working the 12 Steps, it can be used the same way for specific therapy models.

Internal Family Systems Therapy, or IFS, is a psychological theory that looks at an individual as having different "parts" or ego states. This concept reflects the hats and masks mentioned earlier in this text. IFS looks at the role and purpose of individual "parts". These parts make you whole, just as members of a family make up the family as a whole. This model looks into the parts that make up your "internal family". Understanding how and when *wounded* or *protective* parts are triggered gives insight into your internal family's dysfunction.

This is similar to family therapy and examining the function of roles played in the family. The focus on IFS is examining and healing your inner family. Think of it as family therapy for your inner family.

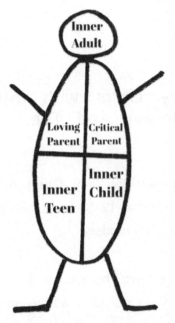

Adult Children of Alcoholics, ACA (also ACoA and ACAODF), has published a workbook titled, The Loving Parent Guidebook (LPG). The LPG has rebranded concepts from IFS and other treatment modalities to fit the ACA terminology. The internal family outlined in the LPG consists of the Inner Child, Inner Teenager, Critical Parent, and Loving Parent.

Suggestions in how to incorporate the Intimacy Gram into these therapies is not meant to be a stand-alone replacement for IFS or the LPG. They are simple instructions on how an Intimacy Gram can be a resource alongside work already being done with these other modalities. Refer back to your completed Intimacy Gram and choose a starting place: pick either realms or relationships.

Realms

If you start with life realms, look at each one and identify your primary ego state, or part, that is activated when you travel through that realm. In the beginning, some parts may stand out more than others; you might be able to quickly identify a "rebellious teenager", "protector", "critical parent", or "victimized inner child." Through a lifetime of survival coping, we may be quite familiar with these identities. You might find one dominant part exists in all of your realms, or you might identify a variety of roles stemming from different realms. It is also possible to have a dominant role present in a realm only to have another role take over when you become stressed or threatened.

In each realm, label the dominant part that "takes over" within that realm. On a scale of 0-100%, rate the percentage of influence, or take over, this part plays in each specific realm. Also rate the percentage of any other existing role(s).

Following through with continued work with an IFS therapist or LPG study group, work on getting better acquainted with that part. Maybe only focus on one part in a specific realm so as to not get overwhelmed.

Periodically, maybe once a month, reflect back on your Intimacy Gram and check for progress in shifting into a healthier ego state. Re-rate the percentage to chart progress and gain better awareness of your growth. As the dysfunctional, or protective, role decreases, you will see an increase in the percentage of the healthier role. Be gentle with yourself (tap into your Loving Parent) when doing this review. If you feel you've made a lack of progress, discuss this with your therapist, sponsor, fellow traveler, or recovery support group.

If a dysfunctional part is ingrained in your role within a specific realm, it might be necessary to replace the realm with a fresh new one. We can work on changing ourselves, but it's really impractical to try to work on changing an entire system. Some environments are just too toxic to facilitate healthy personal growth. If you don't like the ego state that arises in certain dysfunctional realms, it makes more sense, when possible, to replace a toxic realm with one that is healthy.

Example:

As a young therapist, my first internship placement was in a local high school. I entered this situation with a professional, adult part of myself. Unfortunately, this high school was my former high school and I was supervised by my former junior high school counselor. Interactions with my past teachers felt stressed. They saw me as the "B" student who slept through junior year and did not return as a senior. The pre-existing conditions of this realm set me up for failure.

Mr. Silvers, now the head Counselor, consistently told me what I needed to discuss with each student. I felt horribly uncomfortable eating lunch in the cafeteria with the teachers. My inner child initially protected me by withdrawing into my office at lunchtime and eating alone. The kids, however, quickly discovered that I was spending time in the office and sought me out. This evolved into a lunchtime drop in group. I utilized the time, nurturing the kids. However, I was not taking care of myself. This lead to some awkward dynamics within my internship placement.

I loved the kids, but felt being around my former teachers and counselors created an environment which kept me from growing. After two semesters, I asked for a change of assignments.

The following semester, my supervisor placed me in a new school within a different district. He also "sold" me to the school personnel as his "best therapist." This alone set the stage for me to walk in as an *adult.* I trimmed my hair and bought a few new ties; *fake it 'till you make it.*

The staff at the new high school had different expectations of me than my former placement. They respected my ability, making it easier for me to function as an adult/professional. In switching environments, I switched realms. I left a realm that didn't allow me to function with an adult identity without conflict and entered a healthier realm. I developed a successful program at Rancho Alamitos High School that flourished for many years. Part of my success functioning in a healthy *part* could be seen in the friendships that lasted long after I left the assignment.

Moral of the story; if your realm doesn't allow you to grow, move to a different realm.

Relationships

Which relationships are corrupted by ghosts of the past? Start by identifying your most current, problematic relationships. Don't overwhelm yourself. Keep it simple. Choose *one* of these to target first.

With this relationship, identify the part of you that comes into play and takes over when you are around that person: hurt inner child, rebellious teenager, critical parent, or a different, dysfunctional aspect of yourself?

Can you:
- Identify any ghost relationships triggering this part of you?
- Identify the core hurts and feelings that come up?
- Catch yourself and enable yourself to take a time out?
- Identify which intimacy killing factor is at play?

Move Beyond Awareness

If you were able to answer any of the aforementioned questions, take this insight and process it more deeply.

Identifying ghost relationship triggers is a first step in detaching the power that the past has over you. Disengaging from ghosts allows you to live more fully in the present. Understand which ghost relationship stands between you and a specific relationship (or many relationships).

Which painful feelings arise when you are triggered? Tap into the familiarity of these feelings.

Give yourself permission to experience and "be in" these emotions, *so long as they arise in a situation when you cognitively know that you are safe*. Being physically threatened by a spouse or struggling with road rage would be good examples of situations where you need to exercise *self-care* and *take action to keep yourself safe*.

If you are working on healing a *specific relationship* that is affected by past trauma, think of *safe* situations like these: feeling rejected at work by boss or coworker, criticized by a spouse or parent, or reacting to spouse or friend's behavior at a party. Working on reactions to non-specific relationships might be an easier place to start. These examples might include being cut off in traffic, seeing others at work getting more praise and recognition than you, or sitting alone during a holiday. Skills you use to remove ghosts in non-specific relationships can be used when targeting primary people in your life.

Traumatic emotions are stored in an area of the brain responsible to thrust us into immediate action; fight, flight, freeze. As you are triggered in a safe situation, feel these feelings and ask yourself which action they are trying to drive you into. This is how we identify our primary action to react.

A primary core wound is abandonment, or perceived threats, leading to abandonment. We process information in the present through our dysfunctional cognitive filters and magnify our reactions to rejection, disapproval, criticism, and conflict.

Tapping into these feelings and triggers of reactivity, we gain awareness into our patterns. These patterns can go back to early childhood. Once we understand the core and origins we can move into a place of proactivity. This helps reduce impulsivity to react.

Learn to identify the intimacy killing factors that arise when an unhealthy part floods you. As you move more toward a response from a Loving or Nurturing Parent/Self, you will gradually replace these factors with ones which build intimacy.

Keeping your healthy, nurturing, and centered parts in control throughout all realms and relationships is the ultimate goal.

Example:

When I managed the residential treatment facility, clients inside the house often stirred up feelings within my employees. The employees would come to me in distress, telling me that they're triggered and unable to work with a certain individual. I always had to remind them that their job was to work with these people. I would then ask them to think about the aspects of the trigger, how they felt, find any core beliefs that might have come up, and any patterns they've seen, like this, in their life. They would usually return to me in a day or two, explaining which family member they were reminded of, and how that was a trigger mechanism. Once they detached from the ghost relationship, they could begin to work on nurturing themselves during their interactions with the client. They could also express more nurturing and generosity towards the client once they could see them for who they truly were.

Extinguishing triggers keeps you focused in the here-and-now.

Follow the path set before you by your therapist, sponsor, fellow traveler, or LPG group to decrease take-overs and increase the role of your Loving Parent.

Appendix List:

Case Study #1-
The Evolution of Cynthia

I have not seen anyone's diagram shift and evolve as much as Cynthia's. When we met, her life was unmanageable. She had been using heroin for 20 years while raising her 2 children. She was a single mother, fueled by East Coast, Latin blood, and drove with a baseball bat in the back seat of her car. Despite her chaos, she found comfort in the drama and upheaval in her life. This was her *normal*.

Cynthia, or CJ as her friends called her, came to me by referral from her social worker. Her children were out of high school and setting off on their own. At 46, she was dealing with a couple of immune-compromising illnesses and her social worker thought it was time for her to get clean and take better care of herself.

Her relationships were few. Beyond her son and daughter, she had a strained relationship with her mother and limited contact with her social worker. All other acquaintances were drug dealers and the people who associated with them. She estranged herself from most family members years earlier. After her husband passed away, 12 years prior, her drug use increased and she fell into a pattern of isolation.

Her initial Intimacy Gram looked something like this:

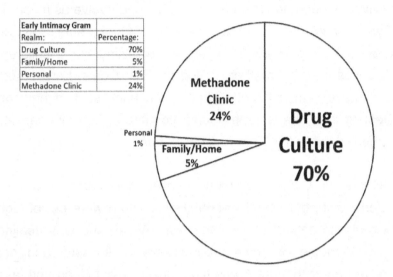

Early Intimacy Gram	
Realm:	Percentage:
Drug Culture	70%
Family/Home	5%
Personal	1%
Methadone Clinic	24%

She lacked a job to give her structure or purpose. As her children grew more independent, the time and energy she spent with them diminished. She traded that time by gaining a stronger foothold in the local using culture. Her clock was centered around the time each morning to get in the methadone dosing line. Most of the friends she would see each morning were the friends she would use heroin or pills with later that day. This cycle went on from day to day and represented her balance.

Her diagram changed instantly when she left the using culture to enter a residential recovery program. She instantly removed one realm and replaced it with another. Not coming into treatment fully of her own accord, she struggled with this transition.

CJ's pie shifted to look more like this:

Shifts in Realms	
Realm:	Percentage:
Treatment	66%
Family	15%
Narcotics Anonymous	10%
Methadone Clinic	5%
Personal	4%

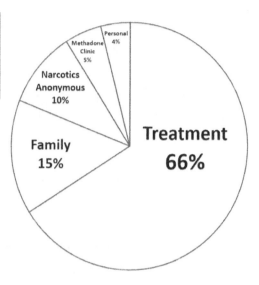

Her life progressed, and her diagram shifted several times over the course of the next year. At times, she fought to let go of old relationships from dysfunctional realms. Her transition took a back and forth, slow progression. She finally let go of old thinking, and her old using friends as the months progressed. While finally moving ahead in treatment, the size of the treatment slice started to lesson. The size of her *family*

slice grew. When her daughter became pregnant, she knew her daughter would not trust her around her child while she was still on methadone (narcotic replacement therapy). She successfully detoxed and tapered off the methadone by the time her granddaughter was born. The *family slice* grew bigger and the methadone clinic slice all but went away.

CJ neared the end of her year-long treatment program by adding a new slice: school. Unfortunately, halfway through her first semester, her health took a bad turn and the *school slice* was replaced with a *medical slice* of doctors and treatments. She worked well to manage and cope with these changes, remaining clean and sober. She fought to keep the Drug/Using Culture realm off of her pie. Her new slices, and newfound involvement with family, helped her to keep her life in balance. She never let go of the treatment slice entirely as she volunteered at the clinic weekly. Once her health had stabilized, she added another new slice to the pie: work. She obtained a job working in Drug Treatment. Her balance had come full circle:

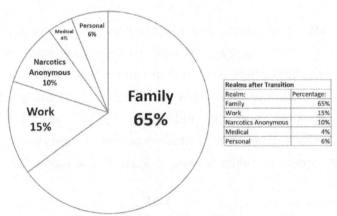

Realms after Transition	
Realm:	Percentage:
Family	65%
Work	15%
Narcotics Anonymous	10%
Medical	4%
Personal	6%

Case Study #2-
Bruce Saves His Family

Bruce sought therapy for the first time in his life at 41. He had the house, the wife, the kids, dog and cat, and an established career. On the surface he looked like the All-American Family Man. With his good looks and desire to help others, he was liked by all.

His initial complaints at the beginning of therapy included work stress leading to lack of sleep. He discussed always feeling behind in his duties. His lack of sleep led to an inability to focus at work, and a resulting irritability when he was at home. His wife felt his stress as he transferred much of his irritation onto her. She was also bothered by his absence from home and insisted he seek therapy.

He presented a very simple Intimacy Gram:

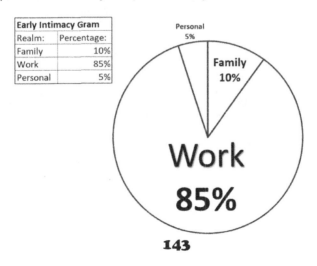

Early Intimacy Gram	
Realm:	Percentage:
Family	10%
Work	85%
Personal	5%

He reported having more balance in his life 2 years before, prior to moving into a bigger home with a bigger mortgage. Back then he spent less time working, which allowed him more leisure time and more balance. Less time at work meant time to attend church with his family, more quality time with his family in general, and the personal time to go running 5 mornings a week.

Bruce presented with feeling burdened by a huge amount of responsibility. He was the kind of man who felt as if he needed to carry the weight of the world on his shoulders. He was third generation Japanese-American. He grew up in a single wage-earner household; dad worked and mom stayed home with the kids. He wished the same for his family. Unfortunately, he was basing his ideals on economics of a time long passed. He reported that his wife had her nursing degree and was willing to work. It was his beliefs that prevented her from doing so.

Bruce did not like seeing the limited realms on his first Intimacy Gram, but this was not what stood out for him. He was both fascinated and challenged by the Factors of Intimacy list. He found many of the factors beyond his comprehension. He even identified feeling embarrassed by not having a grasp of several of these factors. His parents modeled hard work and discipline. They taught him how to have integrity and how to be responsible. They did not teach him how to communicate affection, compassion, and validation. He said that he felt a "hollowness in seeing this that almost bordered shame".

Bruce felt a strong need to "right the wrong". He wanted to grasp these principles and use them to enrich his connection with his wife and kids.

Bruce started by opening communication about finances with his wife. Logistically, cutting down on his hours at the office was possible. He could change his work schedule as he had colleagues to whom he could defer his evening and weekend hours. He wanted to shrink the *work slice* to widen time spent with family. His wife welcomed the changes he proposed. She assured him that financially, she knew they would be fine and welcomed the opportunity to get a part-time position.

It took a couple of months for Bruce to open his schedule. Change did not come overnight. When it did come, he felt a decrease in his stress. He also gained a sense of direction and a goal. As his availability opened up, he started a weekly date night with his wife and game night with the family. He started to coach his son's soccer team. He also set limits with his job that he was not to be on call during those times.

Bruce continued his focus in individual therapy on building his factors of intimacy. He used the time with his wife and his family to implement and build upon these factors. He learned as an adult to develop and maintain emotional connections. In the end, he felt he finally achieved the balance that he failed to get through his old routine and behaviors.

His parting words at the completion of his therapy were, "The Intimacy Gram saved my marriage."

Life Post Therapy	
Realm:	Percentage:
Work	60%
Home/Family	25%
Church	5%
Kid's Sports	5%
Personal	5%

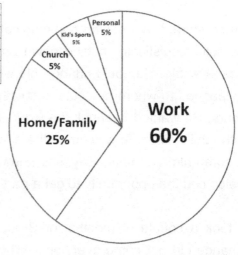

Additional Resources:

Check out these sites on the web for handouts, further instruction, and other related materials:

Website: TheIntimacyGram.com

YouTube:
https://www.youtube.com/@TheIntimacyGram/featured

Look for
The Intimacy Gram
on Facebook and Instagram

The Intimacy Gram

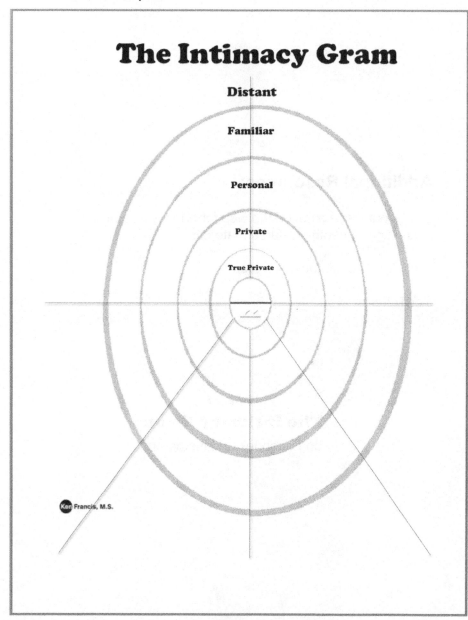

Distant

Familiar

Personal

Private

True Private

Ken Francis, M.S.

The Intimacy Gram

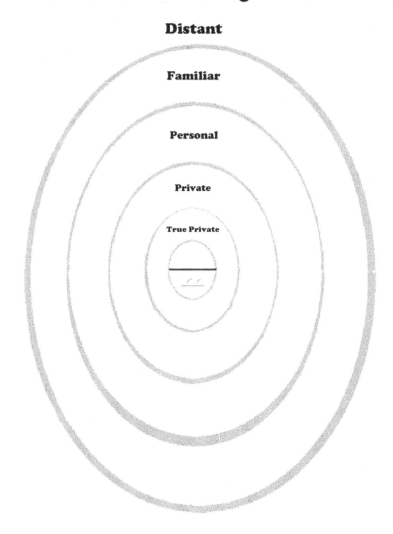

Distant

Familiar

Personal

Private

True Private

Factors of Intimacy Worksheet

Relationship/Name: _____

Factors of Intimacy	Strength of Factor (%)	Notes
Acceptance		
Accessibility/Availability/proximity		
Affection		
Authenticity		
Balance		
Being in the Moment		
Comfort		
Commitment		
Communication		
Compassion		
Compatibility		
Empathy		
Encouragement/Challenge		
Equity		
Forgiveness		
Gratitude/Appreciation		
History		
Honesty		
Humility		
Identification		
Interdependence		
Kinship/Compatibility		
Love		
Loyalty		
Mutual Attraction		
Open-mindedness		
Passion/Attraction		
Patience		
Playfulness		
Respect		
Risk		
Romance		
Security		
Sex		
Shared Background/Experiences		
Shared Beliefs		
Shared Goals		
Shared Humor		
Shared Interests		
Shared Values		
Sincerity		

Support		
Surrender/compromise		
Tolerance		
Touch/Affection		
Transparency		
Trust		
Understanding		
Value		
Vulnerability		
Willingness		

Intimacy Killing Factors	Strength of Factor (%)	Notes
Anger		
Avoidance		
Abuse (physical, sexual, verbal, neglect)		
Blame		
Catastrophizing		
Competition		
Conflict		
Conflict of interest		
Depression		
Discontentment		
Dishonesty		
Disinterest		
Disloyalty		
Distrust		
Envy		
Fear		
Greed		
Hate		
Impatience		
Infidelity		
Irrational thinking		
Irresponsibility		
Lust		
Martyrdom		
Mindreading		
Misrepresentation		
Rationalization		
Resentment		
Selfishness		
Shame		
Smothering (excessive caretaking)		
Vengeance		
Unavailability		

Intimacy Gram Group Check-in/Introductions

What did you do well today?

Who anchored you today?

Attached or avoidant?

Honest or dishonest?

Accepting or critical?

Team player or rebellious?

Forgiving or resentful?

Selfish or selfless?

Indulge or restrain?

Abusive or compassionate?

Patient or impatient?

Realm or factor?

Struggling or secure?

What factor/realm can you improve upon?

ABOUT THE AUTHOR

Ken Francis, MS, is a California licensed Marriage and Family Therapist who has been working with individuals, families, and groups since 1988. He has been teaching the Intimacy Gram in outpatient settings, inpatient settings, and public seminars since 1998. He balances his Intimacy Gram with friends and family from all over the world.

Made in the USA
Las Vegas, NV
05 December 2023

82029029R00094